THE PHILOSOPHY OF LEISURE

The Philosophy of Leisure

Edited by

Tom Winnifrith

Senior Lecturer in English and Comparative Literary Studies
University of Warwick

and

Cyril Barrett

Reader in Philosophy
University of Warwick

St. Martin's Press   New York

First published in the United States of America in 1989

Printed in Hong Kong

ISBN 0–312–02402–9

Library of Congress Cataloging-in-Publication Data
  The philosophy of leisure / edited by Tom Winnifrith and Cyril
  Barrett.
       p. cm.
    Includes index.
    Contents: Introduction / Cyril Barrett—The concept of leisure /
  Cyril Barrett—Leisure: the purpose of life and the nature of
  philosophy / R. T. Allen—Work, leisure, and human needs / Sean
  Sayers—Lived time, leisure, and retirement / Maurice Roche—
  Personal being and the human context of leisure / Alex Gordon—
  Another way of being: leisure and the possibility of privacy /
  Martin Davies—Sport as moral educator / Simon Eassom—Playing
  the game: morality versus leisure / Tom Winnifrith—French
  intellectuals and leisure: the case of Emmanuel Mounier / Brian
  Rigby.
    ISBN 0–312–02402–9: $35.00 (est.)
    1. Leisure. I. Winnifrith, Tom. II. Barrett, Cyril.
  GV14.P47   1989   88–19756
  790'.01'32—dc19   CIP

For Don

Contents

Notes on the Contributors

R. T. Allen is Senior Lecturer in the Faculty of Education at the University of West Indies, Trinidad.

Cyril Barrett is Reader in Philosophy at the University of Warwick, an art critic, and author and editor of books on aesthetics and contemporary art.

Martin Davies is Lecturer in German and French in the School of Modern Languages at Leicester University. He has written a number of articles on German culture of the eighteenth century and European intellectual history of the early twentieth century.

Simon Eassom is a former teacher of physical education with experience of playing and coaching a number of sports at a high standard. He is now Senior Lecturer at Bedford College of Higher Education where he is in charge of teaching philosophy to future education teachers, coaches and administrators.

Alec Gordon teaches linguistics at Vesalius College at Brussels. He has published essays on counter-culture, linguistics and translation theory and in the area of comparative literature, and he is currently writing a critique of contemporary cultural studies.

Brian Rigby is Lecturer in French at the University of Warwick. He has written mainly on French and English literary and political relationships in the late eighteenth and early nineteenth centuries. He is currently working on a book on modern French popular culture.

Maurice Roche is Co-Director of the Policy Studies Centre at Sheffield University and also teaches in the Department of Sociological Studies. He has published in the fields of philosophy, social theory and leisure studies and is currently working on a book on the social theory of 'citizenship'.

Sean Sayers is Lecturer in Philosophy at the University of Kent at Canterbury. His publications include *Reality and Reason* (1985) and (with Richard Norman) *Hegel, Marx and Dialectic* (1980). He is currently writing a book on issues of work and leisure.

Tom Winnifrith is Senior Lecturer in the Department of English and Comparative Literature at the University of Warwick and Director of the European Humanities Research Centre. He has written books on the Brontës and on the Balkans.

Introduction

CYRIL BARRETT

Leisure seems too trivial a subject to be treated philosophically. The philosophy of work, yes: that is serious. But leisure is nothing. It is either a piece of spare time between serious and important or necessary pursuits, or the kind of activities engaged in during this period – leisure activities. What possible philosophical problems could such activities or absence of activity generate?

The first reply to such an objection is that the fact that a subject may seem trivial does not make philosophising about it trivial. Humour, laughter and joking may seem trivial pursuits, yet philosophers such as Bergson and thinkers such as Freud have devoted much space to discussing them.

The second reply is that leisure is more serious than it may at first appear. Of course there is the light-hearted side of leisure – lying on the beach, drinking in the pub, parties, dancing, playing games, watching TV or going to the flicks. But at the other end of the scale some, if not all, of the greatest achievements of mankind have come about precisely because, unlike the rest of the animal kingdom, some of us at least have leisure. Leisure to think, to create, to write, to make useless things. These activities may be regarded as work both by those who engage in them and those who pay for them being thus engaged. This immediately raises the question of what is work and what is leisure; and thereby a philosophical discussion is generated.

In this book we have tended to avoid the rather fruitless task of drawing a strict demarcation between work and leisure. I maintain that any activity can be work in one context and leisure, albeit odd, in another. Accountancy, torture, sheet-metal bashing might not be regarded as normal leisure activities, and yet they have been means of diversion from normal work for some people.

Of course we cannot discuss leisure without reference to work. What we have attempted to do is to realign the two concepts. Dr R. T. Allen and I have attempted to take the concept of leisure back to its classical origins, where work was considered a state inferior to that of leisure. Leisure, according to the ancients, is the proper state of man. Work is what is necessary for survival and a necessary condition for leisure. It is not an end in itself. Leisure is. It is the end, the goal, of human life. At least, that is how we see it.

This may be a reversal of Weber's 'Protestant work ethic'. I think it is. Admirable though that ethic is in many ways, and I mean this sincerely, since it was largely through the work ethic that, led by the United States of America, we owe our present, if unevenly distributed, material prosperity, yet it lacks an end. Work for work's sake makes no sense. If you are a Mother Teresa you work to save the destitute Indian poor. That is not only admirable, it is intelligible. But just to work for the sake of working may have a religious significance for the worker, but it has no significance for the unbeliever.

It may seem that we are tailoring to the times. We are living in an age of unemployment, unemployability and early redundancy. If what we are saying is relevant to the present situation in 1987, so much the better. But this is not what we set out to do. Our main concern is to clarify the concept of leisure and explore its implications. Obviously enforced leisure will play a part in our discussions, but, though, as Sean Sayers says, retirement and redundancy rob leisure of some of its pleasure, for instance the pleasure of having a drink with mates after work, this is not all there is to leisure.

In a sense what we are attempting is to turn the notion of leisure round and put it firmly on its feet as the most serious or, at least, one of the most serious of human activities and occupations.

This, of course, is entirely opposed to the puritanical work ethic which sees leisure as either idleness, which is sinful, or as a necessary break between one period of work and another, a break in which, as with eating and sleeping, one regains the strength to do more work. It is such a view that has created the problem of leisure. Leisure itself is not a problem. It is nothing more or less than the fulfilment of human potential. Of course, one may have to *work at it*. To become a skilled anything – footballer, tennis player, violinist, scientist, writer, philosopher – one has to put in a great deal of hard work: and sustained hard work. But it is leisure for all that. It is fulfilling to the mind, soul and body. It is not drudgery. Compare writing a thesis – about the most exhausting work imaginable, though not always recognised as such – with working at a till or on a factory floor or preparing food or cleaning. What reward does the till girl, the factory worker, the food preparer, the cleaner get? Perhaps the satisfaction of a job well done. Perhaps. But day after day, week after week, month after month? There is work and work. There is work that has been traditionally regarded as leisure *(scholē)* which involves hard work and does not imply idleness – all forms of study and teaching, contemplation and meditation, scientific observation, writing, painting, sculpting, composing and playing music, acting and such like. These activities produce no commercial goods, rarely *physically* improve the environment, leave little lasting mark or trace upon the face of the earth. And yet, along with good statesmanship, a well-regulated family and household, well-regulated living, kindness, generosity and mercy, and love above all, they rank as the highest human values, values that make life worth living for which wealth, prestige, physical prowess, hygiene and efficiency can be sacrificed.

Seen in this context, as the authors of this book see it, leisure is not trivial nor does it need to make any excuses for itself. It is purely and simply part of the way we ought to live. This is how the ancients – the Greeks, the Romans, the Celts, and, doubtless, other sage and mature races – saw things. Leisure is living. The idea that people should be *trained* for leisure is as farcical and laughable as that they should be trained for living. That anyone should suggest such a thing shows how distorted our conception of human nature has become over the last four or five hundred years. Nevertheless that is how things are at present. Leisure has become a problem, the biggest psychological problem after loneliness, and akin to it. Both Sayers and Maurice Roche address themselves in different ways to this. Roche is more optimistic in that he sees people out of work not so much deprived of work as in a new state, that of leisure, without the constraints of work. Sayers sees them as deprived in so far as they have no work in terms of which to contrast their leisure. This in itself might not be a serious problem since even the leisured have chores, and can distinguish between work and leisure proper. But Sayer's point is that they no longer have work-mates. This, I think, is an important point.

In trying to get a balance between work and leisure, however one assigns these terms, it is important neither to exalt one at the expense of the other, nor denigrate one to the advantage of the other. Leisure has a liberating influence, but, as the Marxists stress, so have work and labour. This is a point rightly stressed by Sayers and Alec Gordon. A human being is fulfilled by productive work, even if it is nothing more than washing dishes, scrubbing floors, peeling potatoes or collecting money at a till. Of course we are talking about remunerated work. That may compensate for lack of 'job-satisfaction'. But what of people who have to perform menial and literally unrewarding tasks? Is work liberating for them, and, if not, can they enjoy their enforced leisure?

This is a topic to which none of the authors fully addressed himself. It belongs more properly to the psychology and sociology of leisure than to the concept of leisure itself. These subjects, it is hoped, will be treated in a subsequent volume. However, Roche, in dealing with the mentality of the retired, as distinct from the unemployed or, worse still, the never-having-been-employed, has laid a foundation for such a discussion.

Apart from the relationship of leisure to work there is the question of the quality of leisure itself. This is the subject of discussions by Gordon and Michael Davies. Gordon, as it were, lays the theoretical groundwork, and Davies fleshes out the ideas with rich literary references. In sum, what both are saying is that leisure is deeply personal. It is the situation in which a human being comes closest to his or her self, just as love-making is the situation in which a human being comes closest to another human being, and prayer is the situation in which a human being touches the transcendental, or at least something greater and more mysterious than himself or his fellows. This may at first seem odd, since one associates leisure with corporate activities such as sport, conversation, walks in the country, attending plays and concerts. But leisure can also involve curling up with a good book, solitary strolls, private meditation, writing diaries, and, in general, 'being with oneself': in other words, the almost religious, at least reclusive, aspect of leisure. And yet even the corporate and public aspect of leisure is also, in a strange way, private. In playing games, talking to one's friends, attending plays and concerts, one may be in public, but – provided the games are not compulsory or the attendance at the concert not forced and formal – one is alone, alone with friends, alone in a congenial atmosphere. This is partly what friends are for. They are those human beings with whom one can be alone, alone to oneself: they do not intrude, do not make demands on your attention, can be taken absolutely for granted, so that you are free to be yourself. Paradoxical, perhaps: that one should be most private, most oneself, most at peace with oneself in the presence of other people. But it is a fact for all that. Perhaps it also could be further explored in a volume on the psychology and sociology of leisure.

Finally, there is the moral dimension of leisure. This has been discussed by Stephen Eassom and Tom Winnifrith, but exclusively in terms of sport. Could matters have been otherwise? What moral problems does leisure present? If one takes a utilitarian view that leisure is necessary in order to recoup one's strength for further work – the puritan work ethic – there is no moral problem at all. Indeed, leisure becomes a moral obligation, like washing one's teeth or changing one's underwear regularly. But what if one goes a little further into leisure – dalliance on the sward, perhaps, or a boozy evening in the pub or club, or skiving off to Morocco when you should be at your desk? These do not present moral problems specifically related to leisure. They may relate to dalliance, fecklessness, idleness, boozing, skiving and other irresponsible moral activities; but none of these are specifically related to leisure as such.

Far from seeing leisure as a moral *problem*, I, along with my fellow contributors to this volume, particularly Eassom and Winnifrith, see it as having some moral advantages. They confine themselves to sport. I shall come to that. But first I wish to offer a broader view. What, after all, is moral goodness except the enhancement of life, as Gordon argues at length and Davies ably supports? In moral matters we are very cautious. 'The enhancement of life' is so nebulous, so unclear, that we prefer to talk in the negative – don't kill, don't hurt, don't cheat. Where leisure is concerned it is hard to find 'don'ts'. So, if there is to be a morality of leisure, it has to be positive, with a provisional negative clause 'provided you do not hurt or offend anyone unreasonably' (people can take offence unreasonably too). With these provisos, I feel that any leisure activity is morally good. And even if you happen to be a 'Will-of-God' moralist it is not unreasonable to assume that God wills the enhancement rather than the denegation of human life. This notion could obviously be developed, but nobody in this volume has done so.

And so we come to sport. Sport as a moral educator has long been a British ploy, from Arnold and even before. What is so moral about sport and why is it educative? Fair play, of course. Play well; 'play up, play up and play the game'. Yes, but what has this to do with leisure? It has everything to do with morals, but more to do with war than leisure. Courage, certainly. That is a warlike quality. But justice also. This is the important point. In play one can repent at leisure. But this will not quite do.

If, however, we widen the notion to play in general, not just confine it to regulated play, sports and games, then the moral importance of leisure as an educator may become clearer. Competitive sport may be akin to warfare or to political and commercial rough and tumble, which can be no less vicious and lethal than warfare, but it is not the real thing. It is play. This is not to say that play may not turn vicious and lethal, but when that happens it has ceased to be play, and certainly ceased to be leisure. The wise and sainted Louis IX of France reversed this process. To reduce the effects of internal conflicts in France, a kingdom over which even he still had but a tenuous hold, he confined them to a limited area, where knights could slaughter each other to their hearts' content without molesting the populace. From this evolved tournaments. From duelling has evolved fencing, a harmless pursuit. Thus was created a situation in which people could exercise martial arts, but in a way that was not lethal. And it was a form of leisure. Play (including horseplay) creates the situation in which you may 'play out' the moral virtues – fair play, courage, graciousness in defeat, modesty in victory, mercy and, when required, mercilessness, self-discipline, reliability and trustworthiness, without anyone getting seriously hurt (as a rule).

But matters are more subtle than that. There is a paradox about moral education. To attempt to inculcate moral principles into young children is a waste of time, and to give them so-called moral habits is not to teach them morality at all, because they do not know why they should or should not do what they are told to do. Thus what they do is hardly moral. A robot could do much the same. Eassom believes that sport offers the best opportunity for inculcating moral principles. It may not be clear to a child why he or she should not kick a person who is down or take unfair advantages or cheat or gloat over someone else's misfortune or return blow for blow or sulk or seek revenge – the list is endless – *in real life*, but it might be easier to inculcate these principles in sport, where, after all, 'it is only a game'. The principles once embedded in a concrete and lived situation, which, being inconsequential (or, at least, partly and seemingly so) does not immediately commit the child to anything – he or she can play the game on the hockey field and yet still not play it in everyday life – may, nevertheless, influence its everyday living. 'It is not cricket' is one of the more endearing clichés of the English language. And yet it sums up what Eassom says: are you prepared to do in the boardroom (and, worse still, behind the backs of the directors) or at a union executives' meeting what you would not have done on the cricket, rugger, football or hockey field? Not a wonderful moral criterion, perhaps, but a practical one, one that might give us pause.

There is another cliché: 'The battle of Waterloo was won on the playing fields of Eton'. Like most clichés (which are usually true, since they are mostly truisms), no one has taken the trouble to tell us what happened on the playing fields of Eton that ensured Wellington's rather lucky victory (at least, by his own admission, – 'A close run thing': just not run out?). But it is not difficult to see what is meant. The most obvious moral virtue that sport engenders is courage, physical and moral courage. The greatest asset of a sportsman or woman is the ability to fight on in the face of possible or even imminent defeat. Another is discipline, not falling apart. This is a part of courage, I suppose, but not identical with it. The Irish are strong on courage but, unless they put their minds to it, weak on discipline. The 'team spirit' does not always come easy to them. But it was this that stood the British in good stead in many a scrape, not least Waterloo.

This raises a slight problem. How universal is Eassom's and Winnifrith's notion of sport? Do other countries, can other countries, be morally educated by sport? This is not clear. It might be a subject for a sociological survey. Fair play, playing the game and being a good loser seem such British virtues. They are to be found in certain parts of the former Empire, but hardly in the whole of the Commonwealth. It is doubtful if they are to be found in Latin countries or in Eastern socialist countries or most Third World countries. And yet there are some universal moral principles that can be inculcated by typically British sports: the basic notion of rule-governed behaviour, and such notions as courage in adversity, generosity in victory, graciousness in defeat; and, of course, some sense of justice, if only that it is not unreasonable to be penalised for infringing the rules. Perhaps the conclusion is that each race and nation has specific virtues that are reflected in the way they play their games and that there are also moral principles inculcated by all sport.

However, as Winnifrith points out, much sport as it is played, particularly by professionals, is a moral educator only in so far as it encourages vice. Empirically this may well be true. The desire to win at all costs, by whatever means, within or without the rules, is certainly not a blueprint for good moral behaviour in life. His suggestion by way of counter examples that sport has no effect on moral behaviour is unconvincing. But I do not think that he would wish to push it. However, he is entirely right in saying that to treat sport or games *purely* as a means towards moral education or as a form of combat with either spoils to be gained or an enemy to be defeated, has nothing to do with leisure. Nevertheless, it remains true that sport or games can have a morally educative effect in (and, possibly, only in) the context of leisure.

Winnifrith draws sport back into the fold of leisure by referring to the aesthetics of sport. Indeed, his thesis is that, in so far as sport is leisure, whether played or watched, it must be enjoyed aesthetically. I think this is right. The aesthetics of leisure is probably the aspect most neglected – or, since it is one of our own special interests, taken for granted. It was hoped that Professor Paul Ziff might have contributed on the subject, but he was otherwise committed. However, in yet another volume that we have in mind, on leisure as portrayed in art, music and literature, we may have an opportunity to go more deeply into the aesthetics of leisure. 'Ethics and Aesthetics are one', as Wittgenstein wrote, echoing the thought of the Vienna of his day.

Lastly, there is the social and political aspect of leisure. Brian Rigby has discussed this in the context of recent French philosophical and political thought where it became a political and ideological issue rather than a simple empirical fact between the 1930s and 1960s. The history of leisure makes rather dismal reading for anyone with egalitarian or even liberal democratic inclinations. For centuries slaves, serfs, peasants and workers in industry were severely limited in both leisure time and leisure facilities. In the Middle Ages there were festivals and fairs; there was the tavern or pub; and there was some domestic jollification. But hunting and fresh water fishing were the preserve of royalty, nobility and gentry; and rambling on their lands was trespass. Then the workers in towns fared little better; long hours of work and exhaustion left them incapable of anything more than sleep or Saturday football, cricket or some other sport, either to play or watch, a visit to a music hall, or, still later, the cinema.

It was to remedy this that French political philosophers argued for an egalitarian attitude to leisure: leisure facilities available to all and opportunities to avail of them. Rigby concentrates on the writings of Emmanuel Mounier, the 'personalist' philosopher, who stressed the need for both the communal and personal aspects of leisure, and the serious moral obligation on every section of the community to provide adequate leisure facilities and leisure time. For him, and for other like-minded thinkers, leisure is not the preserve of the few, the élite, the 'leisured class'. Leisure is the right of all.

If this book does nothing more, it at least shows that leisure is not a trivial pursuit; not a poor relation of work; not a gap or vacuum in the turmoil of life to be filled somehow. Leisure is life lived at its fullest, richest, most complete.

Note

The papers which follow, with two exceptions – those by R. T. Allen and Maurice Roche – were read at the conference 'The Philosophy of Leisure', held at the University of Warwick on Saturday, 6 December 1986. There is some repetition of ideas, particularly by those who did not attend the conference, but the editors thought that these should be allowed to stand. If nothing else, this emphasises the remarkable consensus of opinion among the contributors, something that was in no way contrived nor editorially engineered. Whether we are correct or just like-minded people the reader must decide for himself.

1

The Concept of Leisure: Idea and Ideal

CYRIL BARRETT

Of all concepts that of leisure is one of the most intractable. Like the concept of time, in the words of St Augustine, we know what it is when no one asks us, but when they ask what it is, we are hard put to to find an answer.

It is a polar concept, to be sure. That is, it is contrasted with something else – work is the usual candidate. But when we try to define work we find ourselves begging questions about leisure.

From its etymology the word 'leisure' (Gk *scholē*; L *otium*; OF *leisir*, from L *licere*, to allow) seems to be a word with many strands of meaning, not all coextensive with its use, but overlapping with each other in the manner of such words as 'game'. Wittgenstein chose 'game' as an example of a word whose meaning cannot be explained in terms of one common characteristic but by various characteristics which bear family resemblances to one another. He might well have gone a step further and chosen the broader term 'leisure' as his example.

What are these strands of meaning? Pride of place is given to free time, time at one's disposal to do with it what one wills. It would be tempting to make this the defining characteristic were it easy to determine what constitutes free time: freedom from what? Once again work suggests itself. And once again one must ask what is meant by work: what one is paid to do? what one is obliged to do? what one does not like doing? There is no reason why one's free time may not be taken up doing something one is paid to do, such as doing the accounts, or what one is obliged to do, such as mowing the lawn, tiling the bathroom or washing the dishes. These may not normally be regarded as leisure activities, but they are done in one's own time, at one's leisure.

This notion of doing something at one's leisure is another strand in the meaning of leisure. However, it cuts across the notion of free time and work, though perhaps not that of spare time. Thus during working hours as usually understood there may be some things that one does at one's leisure, either when there is *no other pressing business* or one is *taking one's time over them*. That is, one does not feel obliged to do them within a specified time. On the other hand, there may be things that one does in one's free time or leisure hours that one does not do at one's leisure. One may stroll around at one's leisure, but one can hardly play a leisurely game of squash or league rugby against an energetic and vigorous opponent; at least, not if one hopes to win or even give the opponent a decent game. Thus not everything that is done in one's free or leisure time is leisurely; nor are all our leisurely activities done in our free time. On the other hand, that other sense of 'at one's leisure', that is, having no pressing business, does in some sense seem to pervade the concept of leisure. I say 'in some sense' because there may always be some aspect from which one is under pressure when not under it from another.

Closely related to the notions of doing something in one's own time and at one's own pace are the notions of rest, ease, quiet, freedom from employment and occupation; in a word, of doing nothing or nothing in particular. None of these notions is synonymous with leisure. An invalid *resting* on his bed or an infant in its cot is not exactly at leisure. If a workman taking a break lies down on the ground or a housewife puts her feet up after a morning's housework or a tennis player collapses on the grass after a match – that is being at leisure. To be leisure, resting must involve temporarily *desisting from* some activity, physical or mental, whether regarded as work or itself a leisure activity.

If rest suggests repose, *ease* suggests relief – relief from strain, from a burden, from troubles, from constraint: being at ease, standing at ease. But it is clearly not synonymous or coextensive with leisure. Someone engaged in tug-of-war is far from being at ease physically; and the relieving of pain does not connote leisure. Yet, in so far as being at ease implies freedom from constraint, it is fairly central to the notion of leisure.

We speak of enforced idleness – being ill or out of work. Can we speak of *enforced leisure*? What of workers paid without being given work to do and even paid not to work, farmers paid not to cultivate the land? And what of the so-called leisured classes, the idle rich, who do not have to do anything, not even wash or dress themselves? Can the way they spend their time be described as leisure? These are limiting and unusual cases which call for special treatment. But even within these unusual constraints one can distinguish between ways of spending the time that can properly be called leisure and ways that cannot, even though the activities engaged in are identical. It is doubtful whether compulsory games are leisure for those who do not want to play them. And likewise with compulsory gym or walks. The same might be said for recreations and exercises, including games, prescribed by a doctor for the good of one's health. On the other hand, knitting or playing cards, if that is what one wants to do, is leisure, even if done during office hours or in work time. What then of the people who like the games or occupations that are either compulsory or what the doctor ordered? They are doing what they want to do even though they have to do it, and, in some cases, do it at a time not of their choice. It would be odd to say that these ways of spending free time were not leisure.

Thus, *doing what one wants to do*, even if one is constrained to do it, in some way, is a necessary condition for leisure. As it stands it is not a sufficient condition, since someone could do what he or she wanted to do at times when not at leisure, whether raising a family, farming, cabinet-making, nursing, teaching, ballet dancing, professional sport. Professional sport, however, must be distinguished from lucrative sport engaged in, not as a necessity or from greed or ambition, but simply because one wants to do it. Provided the person engaging in it is free from other commitments (legitimately or illegitimately) such sport is leisure. This opens up possibilities. Can any activity that one engages in purely because one wants to do it when free from other commitments be deemed leisure? I shall return to this question.

While still on constraints it should be noted that leisure is rarely free from constraints of some kind. There are social obligations – to attend a party or go to the theatre ('I'm not free tonight') – and there are the rules of games which have to be adhered to. But if these things are what one wants to do; if they are not *tasks* to be performed; above all, if one has freely undertaken to do them: that is leisure.

Out of this discussion emerges another strand of meaning. It is: *doing something for its own sake*, and not for any purpose. Thus to read a book in studying for an exam, to garden in order to earn money, to walk to work as the only means of getting there, to report on a play, film, concert or game for a newspaper, this is not leisure. To read just for the sake of reading, garden just for the sake of gardening, walk for the sake of walking, watch plays, films, games and listen to music just for the sake of watching or listening: that is leisure. Another way of putting this is to say that leisure is essentially a useless way of passing the time. It has no value but the doing of it. That is its value: to require no other.

One might be tempted to substitute for doing something for its own sake, doing it for pleasure. While not incorrect, the notion of pleasure as applied to leisure requires careful handling. Many ways of spending one's leisure are painful in the extreme – competitive cycling, mountaineering, rowing, boxing, gymnastics, wrestling, squash, cross-country running, tug-of-war. Doing them gives pleasure; having done them gives the pleasure of relief and satisfaction; but it would be odd to describe being bashed about a boxing ring as a pleasurable way of spending the time, much less a pleasant one. Enjoyment is probably a better word. There is nothing odd about saying that a tough fight or a taxing climb is enjoyable. But both these words – and there are others, such as fun – concern effects and can be effects of other activities, such as distributing prizes or teaching someone to swim, which need not be leisure activities. Doing something for its own sake comes nearer to telling us what is being done when an activity or inactivity is leisure. Moreover it seems, along with doing what one wants to do, to be almost a sufficient condition for something being leisure. Wanting to do it has to be brought in since walking, and so on, for its own sake would not be leisure if one did not want to do it.

But can every occupation carried on in one's free time for its own sake be regarded as leisure? Some, notably morally commendable actions, are said to be done for their own sake, and one would hardly regard telling the truth, being honest and fair, kind, tolerant, forgiving, hard-working and chaste as leisure activities. But are these actions done for their own sake? They are done without any regard for personal advantage to be sure. But to go about telling the truth, being kind, forgiving *for the sake of it* is not only a formula for becoming a thorough nuisance, but is hardly even moral: it would be a form of self-indulgence, at best.

What of a life devoted to learning and the arts? If the artist or scholar is self-supporting, is he not engaged in an activity purely for its own sake? But if his whole life is devoted to it, how can it be regarded as a leisure activity? Perhaps here we come to something central again. It is the possibility of a whole life being devoted to leisure pursuits. This may sound strange to someone brought up to think of work, whether remunerated or not, being the principal function or *raison d'être* of a human being. True, if we spend a life of leisure it is hard to see what the free time is free from. But this presupposes that there must be some *time* in our life, in our day, when we are not free; some time with which free time is contrasted. But why must this be? This brings us to the question that can no longer be avoided: what is free time?

Let us start with *institutional free time* or declared free time – periods off work, holidays, lunch and tea-breaks, recesses, vacations. This presupposes a fairly regimented life: in the forces, in factories, mines, on ships, in offices, in the classroom, and so on. But it would include both flexible regimes as well as self-imposed inflexible regimes. And within this framework there would be room for 'taken' free time: playing truant, French leave, the delayed lunch, and so forth. And within this framework are also those monks and nuns who do not work for a living, but yet divide their day into a time for prayer, a time for manual work, a time for reading or study, and a time for recreation or pottering – their free time. Whether all that goes on within the period of free time is leisure, or whether only what goes on during this time is – a commonly held view – are questions calling for further discussion.

Cutting across, though not necessarily at odds with institutional free time, is what I shall call '*time free from necessity*'. Some people – slaves, paupers, peasants, puritans – have none of it. There is no time they can call their own. Not only that, they are entirely occupied in providing for the necessities of life, their own life in the first instance, other people's lives and luxuries, which become their necessities, and the abstract concept of doing something productive at all costs and at all times. This latter motivates those of a puritan turn of mind. Others may have no institutional free time, but have time free from necessity. Their whole day need not be devoted to caring for themselves and their dependents. Their free time can be largely when they wish to take it. The *self-employed* and the self-supporting belong to this class. These categories include, for my purposes, besides such self-employed as those engaged in family businesses or private practice, housewives, students, clergy, voluntary workers, scholars, artists and writers on grants. In other words, the gainfully and not-necessarily-gainfully *employed*. No one, not even the *unoccupied* – pre-school children, tramps, the idle rich, the sick and infirm, loafers, prisoners in solitary confinement – are completely free from the necessities of life.

There are some basic necessities – eating, sleeping, finding shelter and clothing – which occupy everyone's time. Then there are moral obligations to be fulfilled which occupy our time – providing for one's dependants, carrying out one's professional duties, fulfilling one's contracts, helping one's neighbour. There are also such light obligations towards one's family, colleagues and community as looking spruce rather than unkempt, keeping the garden trim, and, more importantly, cutting down the thistles before they flower and waft into the neighbours' fields, and suchlike. And finally, there are the self-imposed necessities. The list of these is endless, from gardening and taking care of cats to filling every moment with productive occupations either out of ambition or a feeling of guilt for time 'wasted' or some other ulterior motive. I am not sure that workalcoholics fall into this category. They may. Being productively occupied may be for them a psychological necessity. On the other hand, it may not be a necessity but just what they want to do more than anything else in the whole world.

In this context a life of leisure becomes a possibility; a life in which necessities are kept to a minimum so that most of one's time is free. It is even compatible with institutionalised time, whether self-imposed, as in the life of a writer or artist, or accepted, as in the life of a monk or nun in a contemplative order. Until comparatively recently such a life was, if not the norm of civilised living, the ideal and desideratum. It is not without significance that the word for business or work in Greek and Latin is the negative of leisure (*ascholia* and *negotium*), want, lack or absence of leisure. Those who have busied themselves with the affairs of state, or in fighting wars, or haggling in the market place, or cultivating the land or at their workbench were the unleisured class (*ascholoi*). Aristotle is quite definite about that: 'We conduct business', he says, 'in order to have leisure' (*Nichomachean Ethics*, x 7.6). The pursuits of politics and war seem to be unleisured because they are engaged in for ulterior motives – the defeat of an enemy or to exercise authority, attain honour or the happiness of one's self and one's fellow citizens. In this context Aristotle comes near to giving a definition of leisure when he says that politics and war are aimed at some ulterior end 'and not chosen for their own sakes'. Later he describes leisure as 'freedom from fatigue'. We have here a vision of the status of a human being as properly that of leisure. This may be described as the ideal of leisure. We must now ask how that leisure is to be spent. Are there any specific leisure activities?

We speak of leisure activities: sports, pastimes, hobbies, play, the arts foremost among them. We build leisure centres to house them. Maybe we do this for a good reason. Maybe there is a category of activity which can properly be called 'leisure' activity to which certain activities belong. But on the face of it this would not appear to be so. First, there does not seem to be any activity that is normally designated a leisure activity that cannot in certain circumstances be regarded as being far from a leisure activity. Likewise there are many activities that would not normally be considered leisure activities which in certain contexts must be regarded as such. Let us examine these two classes of activity.

Sports, pastimes, hobbies, play, the arts. Of these, play, including children's play, horseplay, practical joking and the like, all of which have dubious claims to be leisure activities anyway – they are rather distractions, expressions of high spirits, diversions – is the only kind of activity that cannot also be a professional occupation, an activity undertaken out of necessity of some kind. With games this is obvious. There may still be games – shove-halfpenny and tiddley-winks among them – that have not yet become either commercial or political, but they are few. And reporting or commenting on them for the press, radio or television is an irresistible possibility. Of course there are still amateurs and spectators who watch games for the love of the game. But games as such are not exclusively a leisure activity.

Other sports such as hunting, shooting, fishing, sailing, either had their origins in necessity or can be put to use: cliff climbing has been used in scaling cliffs on commando raids. The utilitarian aspect of such pastimes as walking, riding, cycling, touring, flying, and almost all hobbies – gardening, carpentry, collecting, beekeeping – is obvious. In the arts we have professionalism on the part of authors, performers, reporters and critics.

This leaves us with a few possible candidates: contemplation – from just watching the world go by to transcendental meditation, resting and sleep. Rest and sleep can be dealt with summarily. Both are necessary. Contemplation is not usually listed as a leisure activity and facilities are rarely made available for it: nor are they necessary. Aristotle ranked it high among leisure activities, but what he had in mind was the cultivation of the intellect, which can certainly be professional. Religious and transcendental meditation is hardly leisure, though it may require time free from necessity in which to do it. This leaves watching the world go by. If it entails observing one's fellow or other natural objects, this could be useful for a writer or an artist. So we are finally left with aimless hanging around, virtually doing nothing. This can hardly be regarded as an activity, much less a leisure activity. It is what Aristotle would have called idleness, which he distinguished from leisure. For him leisure involves activity: it is essentially active.

This calls for a brief excursus. Idling at work we are all familiar with. Those who adhere to the work ethic would regard free time spent aimlessly and profitlessly as idleness. The ancients and medievals, Seneca and Aquinas in particular, regarded idleness (*accidia*, sloth) as a worthless and frivolous activity. For Seneca it consisted of gossip, the pursuit of trivial knowledge, sunbathing and the like. In a word, the pursuits of the idle rich. In this view – and it too is an ethical view – so far are these pursuits from not being leisure; they render those who indulge in them incapable of enjoying the full enrichment of leisure.

If there is no activity – with the possible exception of contemplation – which is exclusively a leisure activity, is there any activity that could not, under any circumstances, be a leisure activity?

Certain forms of manual work – gardening and carpentry – have long been accepted as leisure activities. Is there any form of manual work that would be incompatible with leisure? If leisure is understood as time spent in unnecessary work that one wants to do, then it is hard to see how even coal mining, sheet metal bashing and the like can be ruled out. It could be argued that it cannot be ruled out even on the grounds of spiritual value if clearing forests and hill farming – work engaged in by monks – can be regarded as compatible with a contemplative life.

But what of responsible work such as that of a surgeon or nurse, soldier, policeman, judge, prison warder, dustman, public administrator? These admittedly are unlikely leisure activities. And, of course, a person engaging in them would have to be qualified and authorised. But it is not unusual for a surgeon on vacation to perform operations or for the local squire or lord to act as a magistrate or enter politics. These activities would be a way of passing the time that made a nice change from games, reading, conversation or contemplation. It could even be remunerated like professional sport, but would have to entered upon voluntarily.

Aristotle would have objected to this on the grounds that these activities are essentially purposive. They are engaged in not for their own sake but for some ulterior purpose. He singles out soldiering and says 'a man would be thought utterly blood-thirsty if he declared war on a friendly state for the sake of causing battles and massacres (*Nicomachean Ethics*, x 7.6). This, however, is a moral stricture which does not affect the issue. What is at issue is whether an activity that is purposive of its nature can be engaged in for its own sake, not whether it should be. It might be said that if something purposive is entered into for its own sake one has to be prepared to disregard the consequences. It is rather like playing the game for its own sake which is taken to mean not caring whether one wins or loses. This may be all right in gardening, carpentry or cooking, where it does not matter whether the plants come up, the grafting takes, the table stands on its legs, the Yorkshire pudding goes flat or rises, but it will not do in politics, warfare and, still less, in surgery. This is one way of looking at engaging in a purposive activity for its own sake. From the moral point of view it may be reprehensible. One should not play at or make a game of warfare, politics or surgery. But the force of this moral stricture is precisely that these activities are being treated as, or as though they were, leisure activities. In being thus they are being deflected from their true purpose and their nature is distorted. Nevertheless, it has to be conceded that, however reprehensible this may be, they remain leisure activities.

But can purposive activities not both fulfil their role, be undertaken seriously and still be pursued for their own sake and not for the sake of their end and purpose? In other words, can we not distinguish between the purpose of the activity and the purpose of the person engaged in the activity? Someone who pursues a purposive activity for its own sake does not necessarily frustrate that purpose. A person engaged in politics for its own sake can be as keen on furthering the welfare of the citizens as someone who is in politics for the sole purpose of furthering their welfare; a soldier of fortune may be as keen on defeating the enemy for the sake of it as a patriot who must defeat the enemy at all cost; the surgeon who performs an operation simply for the sake of performing his art need be no less keen on saving the life of the patient than the surgeon whose duty it is to perform the operation or who, for some other reason, is committed to saving the life of the patient.

Finally, what of sadistic and gross sexual activities? Can these be regarded as leisure activities? Within a non-normative description of leisure activity they must be included. Historically, the infliction of pain on humans and animals has long been a leisure activity and watching it for just as long. Sometimes it is indulged in out of hatred, revenge, to extort information, as a deterrent or for some other reason. But as often as not it is indulged in for its own sake. Sexual abuses, to say nothing of the varieties of sexual indulgences, are even more often indulged in for their own sake.

So much for the idea, or rather the ideas, of leisure. They are not so much conflicting as overlapping or shading from one into another. Something can be excluded from the concept of leisure or included by a variety of criteria. But there remains a centre or core of the idea which I shall call the ideal of leisure. This commands a wide measure of agreement, if not absolute unanimity.

If, on the one hand, there is no single kind of activity or sets of activities that are exclusively leisure activities, and on the other hand, there is no activity that cannot, in given circumstances and by a not unreasonable set of criteria, be regarded as a leisure activity, this does not mean that there is not a set of activities that are *per se*, paradigmatically and properly (in the Latin sense) leisure activities. They represent the ideal way of spending one's leisure.

Once again we must turn to the Greeks and, in particular, to Aristotle. We also return to those activities that have already been put forward as candidates for activities that are essentially leisure activities, but now in inverse order: contemplation, the arts, free play, hobbies, pastimes and sport.

Consider contemplation; and by this I understand not only meditation, pondering deeply, and scholarly pursuits, but also listening to music, watching plays, observing nature and even taking an intelligent interest in almost anything for its own sake. This might be too wide for Aristotle. No matter; what he says still applies. And what he says is that human happiness, which distinguishes humans from other animals, is 'some form of contemplation'; they are coextensive. Contemplation is the activity of the gods who are supremely happy. Contemplation, in Aristotle's view is superior to moral activities which also conduce to happiness, but only secondarily. We cannot imagine the gods 'making contracts and restoring deposits and all that sort of thing'. His lengthy argument is summed up thus:

> that which is best and most pleasant for each creature is that which is proper to the nature of each; accordingly the life of the intellect is the best and pleasantest life for man, inasmuch as the intellect more than anything else is man; therefore this life will be the happiest.
>
> (*Nicomachean Ethics*, x 7.9)

Following this through one might put not only reading, looking at and listening to works of art on a par with producing or performing them as leisure activities, but likewise watching play, whether free or formal – dancing, figure-skating – or rule governed (games), would be on a par with performance.

One could approach these activities from the opposite angle, that of activity rather than contemplation. Here the emphasis would be on play or free and creative activity as the most rewarding, the most humanly fulfilling, in Aristotelian terms, the most pleasant and happiest activities. Meditation, artistic production, creative thought, invention, imaginative play would thus be seen as leisure activities *par excellence* and *per se*. *Per accidens* they may be activities of necessity, just as activities of necessity may *per accidens* be leisure activities.

This, as Wittgenstein would say, leaves everything as it is: leisure centres, if we include monasteries and retreats, schools, theatres, museums, playgrounds and playing fields, are places of leisure *per se*. Factories and offices and farms are places of leisure *per accidens*.

It would be a mistake, however, to accept the Aristotelian picture as it stood. It is not simply that leisure in his day, given the social structure, and the absence of factories and offices, was the preserve of the few, but that it was seen in the conceptual scheme bred of this social structure: the rigid distinction between the liberal and mechanical arts. This blinded the ancients and medievals to the cultural and emancipatory value of non-leisured activities.

So, just as it is a mistake to regard leisure as time off from the principle activity of a human being, work; so it is a mistake to regard leisure as a repository of all cultural and emancipatory values. And one further mistake follows from these two: that of talking about educating people for leisure. The people for whom leisure, unemployment or retirement is a problem would have found their unskilled labour a problem in the first place. For them it was only a job, something to do in order to make money. For such people leisure-time is unlikely to be more than time to be filled in somehow, not an opportunity to continue the process of self-fulfilment. It is hard to see what education for leisure could be other than simply education. But that is a problem for the educators.

One last point, reverting to what has been said before: there can be no absolute leisure. 'Leisure', as I said at the beginning, is a relative term. Even if it is the positive (*schole, otium*) as against the negative (*ascholia, negotium*) pole of the relationship, it is relative for all that. But, if a life of leisure is meaningless in so far as there is nothing with which to contrast it, leisure as simply living without any constraints or necessities – that is, with the possibility but not actuality of constraints and necessities – is not meaningless. Whether this is possible for human beings is an empirical, not a conceptual, question; and I do not wish to preempt any future empirical discussions we may have on the subject.

2

Leisure: the Purpose of Life and the Nature of Philosophy

R. T. ALLEN

LEISURE, WORK AND EDUCATION

The classic conception of leisure, which endured through the Middle Ages, has been effectively restated in our times by Dr Josef Pieper in his *Leisure: The Basis of Culture* (with which is also and appropriately published his reflections on the nature of philosophy itself: 'The Philosophic Act'). I propose to develop that account in certain respects and in relation to pervasive features of contemporary life, to suggest certain modifications of it, and to show in my own way how leisure and philosophy are intimately connected with each other and with the question of the meaning of life.

Many of us today will think of leisure as free time, which is set over and against work, in the sense of an occupation or employment, as time off from work. It is therefore defined privatively as time unoccupied by work, and not positively as having an intrinsic character of its own. Thus arises a modern problem, or a problem acute in the modern world, of what to do with free time now that working hours are much shorter for many people, as also is the working life, while others have the problem of being without gainful employment. Today, whether or not it was so in the past, we mostly see life in terms of work and not-work or free time, and, though we may think that our activities fall clearly into the one or the other, they are nearly all related to work precisely because they are either work or not-work. This domination by work shows itself poignantly when men, and I stress the gender, have no work to do in times of unemployment or in retirement. Many find themselves at a loose end and with nothing to do, and they are not used to that. If unemployed, they feel useless, and when retired feel finished. Women always have the house to look after and meals to get, but they too can feel the emptiness and frustration of less to do when the children have grown up and left home. Notice how often the husband dies comparatively early after retirement, for he has nothing to do, whereas the wife carries on with the housework and her other interests. Think, too, of how often people complain of boredom, of having nothing to do, especially the young, who, as well as having more things done for them today, also are kept away from work for much longer. Many of us appear to assume that the business of life is work.

When that assumption is made, free time is empty or filled by more work or with reference to work. I read in the newspaper that the Japanese are reluctant to take holidays, and take only short ones. On the shop-floor, many are interested in overtime, which, of course, is paid at higher rates. Many senior people in business, and in academic life, take home work in the evenings and work at the week-ends, when at least some of them could delegate much of it. And even those activities of free-time which are not yet more work may be taken up because of work, as relaxation from it and therefore as recreation for it. Often there are other motives even more directly related to work, such as playing golf in order to make useful business contacts. And we often think of free time as the time for relaxation and recreation: relaxation from work and recreation for it; so that, even when it is not occupied by extra work, free time is used for the purposes of work, for making us able to work again and better.

This attitude, which flies from free time back to work or uses it for work, is one of 'total work'. I take that phrase from Dr Pieper who writes of the 'state of total work', which he experiencd under the Nazis. Others still experience it under Communism, and yet others would experience it in 'third-world' states whose rulers have grandiose plans for 'development', if those plans were effectively implemented. A state of total work is one in which everyone is a functionary, defined by his position in the state machine and valued according to his contribution in producing its intended product. Such a state has no place for those who are useless – useless, that is, in terms of producing the results desired by its rulers. Thus literature, the arts and academic pursuits have to serve the declared aims of the state, and so they become propaganda or useful research. (With Dr Pieper let us note the inherent connection between leisure and freedom from total work, on the one hand, and philosophy, on the other: that without it philosophy is required only to elaborate, defend and demonstrate the ideology of the total state.)[2] The attitude of mind which manifests itself in totalitarian regimes, where those at the top compel the rest to conform to it, can also appear in individuals and groups elsewhere, and can dominate a society, without the need for coercion and without one inclusive plan or goal. Quite freely people may devote themselves to work, and each individual or group to its chosen work or function, with only the spontaneous co-ordination of the market. Something like that seems to be happening in Japan.

Consequently, we may take this attitude to be the normal one, not only in the sense of 'average' or 'prevailing', but in that of 'normative' or 'correct'. If so, as Dr Pieper remarks, we may be unable to understand Aristotle's statement that 'we work in order to have leisure'.[3] Indeed, in Greek and in Latin, the positive term is 'leisure' (*scholē, otium*) and for 'work' in the contrasting sense, there was only the privative (*ascholia, negotium*), exactly the reverse of the usual way of thinking and speaking today. But, if by 'work' we mean that which we have to do to provide for the necessities of life, then it is the current attitude which is abnormal. We, or many of us, have forgotten why we work and have made it the end of life and not the means.

To recapture the classical, and normal, outlook, we have to think of leisure as time, not so much free from work, but free for what is really worth doing. Leisure therefore raises the question of the purpose of human life, of man's end or good, of what is really worthwhile. And, if we have no idea of what that is, or despair of ever finding it, we can cover our lack of direction by redoubling our efforts to achieve the means, which is how Santayana defined 'fanaticism'. We find a parallel to this in some political activists who deliberately refuse to think about what they are ultimately aiming at and focus wholly upon the proximate targets of winning the next election or bringing in the Revolution. Perhaps our feverish activity hides a secret despair about finding anything really worth working for. Certainly, we meet individuals who have become so engrossed in earning a living and more that they have ceased to think what it is all for, and so suddenly they find that much of life has passed them by, that, for example, their children have grown up unnoticed.

So, then, what is worthwhile and worth working for? It is here, I suggest, that the classical tradition needs certain amendments. The Aristotelian account answers *contemplation*: knowing for its own sake.[4] From that follows the traditional distinction of liberal and servile arts, those which are pursued for their own sakes and those for that which we can produce or procure by means of them. Liberal education is thus an education in the liberal arts and a preparation for the right use of one's leisure. But, under the influence of Aristotle or of certain misreadings of him, it has become customary to think of liberal arts and liberal education in terms, not of an aim, but of a content: liberal arts or liberal studies are taken to be things such as history, literary studies, pure science and philosophy, and a liberal education to be one which is the study of those subjects. Thus they are restricted to *knowing* and to the knowing and learning of a particular range of items. One can see this still at work in some contemporary accounts of education.[5] But such a conception offers nothing to those who lack interest in and the capacity for such subjects, which is precisely the dilemma of education today, now that formal education for all to the age of 16 has been decreed to be obligatory and little thought has been given as to what is to be done with those detained in schools who either do not wish to be there or who cannot cope even with watered down versions of the customary curriculum.[6]

It is, I suggest, a mistake to think of leisure and liberal pursuits in terms of a fixed and determinate content. Aristotle, or his interpreters, were misled into thinking that the value of a productive art lies wholly in that of its product, and that, in turn as being its commercial value. Some arts may be inherently 'servile' in having no value apart from what they bring about, but many usually so classified are not necessarily servile. For example, the productive arts and crafts of carpentry, cobbling, building and smithing can be practised at least partly for their own sakes, for the joy of making, for delight in the exercise of mastery and skill, and for the satisfaction of producing a well-made article. Their value is not simply that of the selling-price of the furniture, shoes, buildings and implements made. Hence in turn they can be part of a liberal education if the emphasis is placed on attention to standards and delight in skill and making things well, and so upon the intrinsic satisfactions which they afford to those who practise them. Some productive arts, like types of engineering, may be too large in scale and too costly to be practised for their own sakes, except in the form of nationalised industries supported by massive subsidies and agriculture in the EEC which piles up millions of tons of unwanted food. But this is an accident, not something essential: after all, there is the hobby of model engineering. Can we then say that everything could be practised for its own sake? Now there are some occupations which appear so disagreeable or so empty and boring that people will engage in them only for the cash reward which they bring, and will not engage in them or in some modified form of them for any other reason.

But, generally, for jobs to be well done, those doing them must find some interest in their work. This is the error of a purely instrumental, utilitarian and mercenary attitude to work: that looking as it is such terms results in it being less well done. Thus, whereas Aristotle said that we make war for the sake of peace,[7] Valdimir Soloviev saw that the professional soldier, who may be regarded purely instrumentally by others, must like the military life partly for its own sake.[8] This brings us to another error of the modern world: of seeing jobs purely as jobs and means of earning money, and not as ingredients in a characteristic way of life. Doubtless there were many in the past who performed their work because it was the only type of work available, just as there are today many who find an intrinsic interest in their work or in the company of those with whom they work. It is the isolated, narrow and repetitive work of the machine-shop or assembly line which most clearly shows the reduction of work to mere work for the sake of money only. That clearly is servile work, from which automation can deliver us, but work and useful arts are not necessarily nor wholly servile.

So far we have been using 'work' to mean 'mere work', 'labour for obtaining the necessities of life'. But the word has other and wider meanings, such as 'task', wherin it can refer to things done for their own sakes, and include 'vocation' as well as 'occupation'. On a purely verbal level, Eric Gill contradicted Aristotle in placing emphasis on man's work.[9] But it is apparent that he was not speaking of mere work, but something of intrinsic value and offering opportunities and demands for conscientiousness, attention to standards, a job well done, and the fulfilment of some of the deepest needs of man. One might say that it was unrealistic, either today or in the past, to think that all men could enjoy what was available to the master craftsman, Gill's model for man at work. But even more unrealistic was Aristotle's ideal of the research scholar and scientist, still upheld by the educational theorists referred to earlier.

The reduction of work to mere work illuminates the problems listed above. On the one hand, holding such an attitude some people paradoxically are dominated by work, for they have lost any sense of purpose in life and so continue to pile up means, or merely occupy their time, without any thought as to what it is all for. On the other hand, others may appear to do the same thing, but in fact do find an interest in their work, and are not simply concerned with its monetary rewards. For example, it may be the case that some people, who are successful in business, regard their income more as a sign of their prowess than as money to be spent on other things, otherwise why would they continue to earn more and more when it is taxed to vanishing point? It may be the case that, whether or not they realise it, people devoted in this way to their work might find deeper satisfactions if they were to turn to other things as well, and so exercise other aspects of their human nature.

Here we can return to the Platonic rather than the specifically Aristotelian elements in the classical account. Dr Pieper for one of his epigraphs quotes *Laws* 635cd, on the gods pitying mankind, born to toil, and preserving the habits built up by correct education in childhood by providing and joining in feasts with men. And with that we may associate Plato's whole conception of human life and education in the *Laws*: as the playing of the 'serious games' or 'finest games' of art and worship (803c-e), in contrast to the cultureless life of an armed camp as lived in Sparta and Crete (666de) and the lust for wealth that leaves no time for anything else (831c). Such a conception offers more than the intellectualist ideal of Aristotle and contemporary theorists of liberal education. To be sure, Plato sees the life of his imaginary colonists as one of work in the fields or in the house followed by 'serious games' in the evening, the former making possible the latter: he did not see how servile arts can be liberalised by an attitude which sees them as more than mere work, such that it can even make 'drudgery divine' –

> Who sweeps a room as for Thy laws,
> Makes that and th'action fine.

But our problem today is that a commercially produced culture for the masses, which is largely undemanding and passively received, has replaced the spontaneous folk culture which Plato took up and modified for his model city. Thus our sports are now mostly spectator sports played by professionals which the rest of us watch, and likewise our other arts and entertainments, with which we may contrast life during the latter half of the last century and up to 1914, when in every town and many villages there were cricket and football teams and other societies and clubs in a higher proportion to the population than today. If work is too much mere work, so also is leisure too much relaxation.

LEISURE AND THE MEANING OF LIFE

But before we imitate the American scout-master, depicted in *The New Yorker*, who said 'Take a break and I want to see no slacking', we would do well to pay attention to another element in Dr Pieper's restatement of the classical conception, signalled by his other epigraph, 'Have leisure and know that I am God' (Psalm 46:10). Leisure and work we have seen to be defined, not by what is done, but by why it is done and the inner attitude with which it is done. At the centre of the attitude which defines leisure is a capacity for silence, listening and receiving. Now that attitude of waiting and listening can be overlaid by excessive activity of a superficial sort in both work and what we may well take at first sight to be leisure. Just as we can work to fill up the felt emptiness of life, so too can we fill up our free time with movement and noise, especially the latter today. If there is nothing really worthwhile in life, then we can busy ourselves with distractions and diversions, the problem of many, especially women, in the leisured classes of previous ages – the men could take up work, in the wider sense, and careers in politics or the army. Leisure, then, declines to mere amusement, time-filling, and becomes, like work and perhaps even more so, something to be got through. If what we hear in our hearts is nothing, or if we fear that we shall hear nothing, then we may well flee that empty silence. Leisure and the attitude that defines it depends upon a belief that there is something truly worthwhile and fulfilling in life, and thus involves a waiting and listening for it.

It is easy to ridicule Romantic poetry, as in the early Wordsworth, of asking for a 'wise passiveness', especially when we are told that

> One impulse from a vernal wood
> Can tell you more of man,
> Or moral evil and of good,
> than all the sages can.

But it did have an important point to make, though it looked for the answer in a generally inappropriate direction, and, as Irving Babbitt complained, was spiritually lazy.[10] Yet there is need to be still, silent and actively listening and waiting, in order to receive, and not to blot out with mere work, noise, distractions, political fanaticism, drugs, gossip, immersion in technicalities (the professional distraction of recent philosophy which gave up the traditional search for wisdom about the world, the good and the right conduct of life) and the like, the message of what Heraclitus, quoted by Dr Pieper, called the 'essence of things'.

This brings us back to the question of the meaning of life. If 'all is vanity', then so is leisure, for, then, what is there for us to do for its own sake, to be the centre of our lives, and to be what we work for? All may be in vain if either nothing has value in itself or if things have a *prima facie* value which is negated by the futility of pursuing them. In both cases life and leisure are pointless. Thus if the value of the items mentioned above, and of everything else, is denied, then leisure, and education for it, become impossible. Equally, they become futile or ultimately meaningless if such things are finally insufficient and are more distractions from life's meaninglessness than its true meaning. Thus we have two questions: (a) Does anything have a real value? (b) If so, is the nature of the world such as to make its pursuit really worthwhile? These are questions of value and of fact, and a positive answer to the question of life's meaning requires a positive answer to both. The answers to each vary considerably, and so, therefore, do their combinations in answer to the question of life's meaning. In particular, there is the division between those who answer (a) in terms of ordinary mundane interests and activities and those who think that such are insufficient. The former will not regard a Secularist account of the world and human life as therefore undermining the worthwhileness of what they regard as valuable, whereas the latter will do so, and, according to what they believe to be the facts of human destiny and the world, will hopefully look beyond this world or this life or despair of life having any real meaning. It is in terms of this division that recent discussions, with one exception, have been conducted.[11] Let us look briefly at three of them.

Professor Kurt Baier argues that it is wrong to conclude that 'there can be no purpose *in* life because there is no purpose *of* life: that men cannot themselves adopt and achieve purposes because *man*, unlike a robot, or a watchdog, is not a creature with a purpose'.[12] Life, he continues, is falsely judged to be meaningless because it is held that there are three conditions for it to be meaningful, and that the universe satisfies none of them: namely, that the universe is intelligible; that life has a purpose; and that all men's hopes and desires can ultimately be satisfied. Yet it can be meaningful if not all of these conditions are met: and, further, death is irrelevant, for, if life is worthwhile, then it is so no matter how short.[13]

Again, Professor P. Edwards, starting with the pessimistic conclusions of Schopenhauer, Tolstoy and Clarence Darrow, argues positively that, if death is bad because it terminates life, then it can be so only because life is good; that, if life is not good, then death is not bad: and so in either case death cannot be preferable to life.[14] He distinguishes between the cosmic and the particular or terrestrial meanings of life, and asserts a denial of the former does not entail a denial of the latter. If life has a meaning for someone, then it has a meaning. And the pessimist sets up special standards for life to be worthwhile, but it is wrong to conclude that, if it is not worthwhle by those standards, it is therefore not worthwhile by ordinary ones, which still guide life, even that of the pessimist.[15]

In the longest of recent discussions, Professor K. Brittan distinguishes two related questions: (i) Why does the universe exist? Why does something exist rather than nothing? or, why the things which we discover and not other things? (ii) why do I exist? Do I exist for some purpose, and, if so, how am I to discover it?[16] And these questions are implicated in answering, What is the meaning of life? If it is felt that it is not enough for us to be able to find some things which are worthwhile and which we can make our aim (what I call an internal meaning), but require a goal set before us by an external power which can be accepted as worthwhile on its own account (an external meaning).[17] In chapters 2 to 4, he reviews three authoritative answers (each of which is a fragment of that of Christian Theism): that God has a beneficent plan for the world which requires each of us to play his part, that the world is the expression of God's glory, and that we exist now to prepare ourselves for another life; a metaphysical (that is, philosophcal) answer: that we are to know and understand the truth, and especially, in its Rationalist form, that we can know that there is a full and necessary reason why the world exists as it does; some informal answers: work, living for an institution, family, serving others, to be oneself, and pleasure. He does not quite endorse any of these and definitely rejects some.

In Chapter 8 he gives his own answer. For life to have a meaning: (a) we must be able to make and be guided by our own general decisions, appealing to common standards, and life would have no meaning if we could not identify mistakes (a Wittgensteinian argument against private languages), for to reject having rules in common with others to isolate oneself, to pose as the only person or non-person, and so for life to have no meaning; (b) one's own life must matter, and life generally matters because a person's life may matter to him; (c) people must or may matter to each other; and (d) in an individual life there must be a possibility of a particular pattern, which adds up to something, and which one can look for, accept and be guided by, though not all the time. As for the meaning of life in the world at large, his answer is, first, that there must be a boundary between the self and the world (from Chapter 6), and secondly, that we can know that the world permits the existence of persons who achieve the four conditions just stated.

In the last chapter he considers the objection that this is not enough, that there must be a plan for the whole world, that we find it, and that it will be accomplished. Such an answer would turn the hypothetical conditions set out in Chapter 8 into categorical ones. He takes such an answer to be a religious (and Theist) one, but tends to interpret religion as either a matter of intra-mundane attitudes or as a rather crude and voluntaristic transcendentalism; for example, that good is simply what God arbitrarily wills, and that living for Judgement Day means setting aside all considerations of this life (rather than rightly living through them). The religious (Theist) answer is not quite rejected but he does imply that the one given in Chapter 8 is sufficient.

We observe a certain broad similarity among these discussions, an argument or implication that, although the world lacks or may lack an inherent meaning which would give a definitive guide and Way to men, life can still have a meaning and be worthwhile in that we, or some of us, can find each his own meaning and worthwhile goals and purposes within it. There is or may be no *one, essential and common* meaning to life, but there can be *meanings* which we each find for ourselves. These answers are similar to the notion of rational autonomy, prominent in the contemporary philosophy of education,[18] that, since the world sets us no Way, we are to teach the young to work out their own for and by themselves. So, too, we may presume, these discussions imply that we each can, and perhaps should, be taught how to look for our own meanings in life, those things which we find to be worthwhile and significant despite the lack of any wider and given meaning and the fact of death.

Professor R. Nozick's is both the most philosophically sophisticated and wide-ranging of recent discussions, and presents another possibility. He criticises Edwards's arguments (parallel to that of Baier) about the irrelevance of death, and formulates his own notion of meaning as the transcending of limits. The meaning of life would apparently lie in something outside of which we cannot even imaginatively stand, something entirely unlimited. This brings Nozick to his notion of the *Ein Sof* – 'without limit or end' (in Hebrew). That which is unlimited cannot be linked to something else, and so the question of its meaning cannot arise, for the one presupposition of that question, that there be something external to the object in question, is not satisfied. There is no answer to 'What is the meaning of the unlimited,' but there is no question either. It transcends the distinction between meaning and meaninglessness, and also between importance and unimportance. Yet how can linking up with it give meaning to our lives? Only if the *Ein Sof* can be its own meaning and if nothing else can. For finite beings meaning involves external connections in transcending limits, and such meaning can be undercut by a yet wider context, which, however, includes that meaning. But there is nothing outside the *Ein Sof*, and so nothing to which it could be connected and which could undercut its meaning. It therefore stands as its own meaning. But must questions about meaning stop at the widest actual context, even though it would be logically possible for a yet wider one to exist, or can they stop only at the unlimited, at that which nothing else could include or undercut? Nozick thinks that the answer is unclear but that there is a push in favour of that which is unlimited in principle. How, then, can it give meaning to our lives? either by ways of linking up to it (but why some and not others?: Nozick does not pursue that question); or by ourselves being one with the unlimited, as in (Advaita) Vedantism. But the latter possibility presents the puzzle of why the all-inclusive substance is in the process of becoming self-concious (through men) and why it is ignorant for the moment – 'if it's so rich, how come it isn't smart?) And in a footnote here he wonders how really inspiring is Hegel's *Geist* which needs us in order to be self-conscious: 'Would you join a country club that *needs* you as a member?' (*Philosophical explanations*, pp. 606–7). But perhaps the process is itself part of the total perfection – a perfect state conjoined with a perfect process. The world-process would then be the way in which Brahman (or the Absolute) overcomes its last limitations as Brahman (or the Absolute), as Sat Chit Ananda – existence, consciousness, bliss: Brahman sends forth the world in order to come slowly to an awareness of its true and perfect nature. But does such an unlimited and all-inclusive being actually exist? Nozick discounts philosophical arguments for it but thinks that reports of mystical experiences carry some weight.[19]

Nozick presents possibilities rather than advancing one definite answer: there is meaning in transcending limits, but that itself is limited, and we may wish for more; and, if we do, he provides a notion which could make the fulfilment of that desire possible. This raises the question of motives in philosophy. He imagines the objection that, if life can have meaning only if there is an unlimited being, perhaps there is no such being and so no meaning in life, and that we should not think that, because life cannot have meaning without it, this is therefore a reason to think that there is such a being. But does such maintenance of rigorous intellectual standards, not yielding to any temptation to be influenced by our hopes and fears, itself have any *meaning*?[20]

In these discussions, save for Nozick's , men are viewed individually, and each is seen as finding or creating his own meaning in life. There is no common and essential meaning, save only the possibility of each finding his own in secular pursuits and goals. But others have viewed men collectively and so have seen the human race as creating a meaning or having purpose which is therefore internal to the race but extraneous to the individual. For example, Hegel sees men as the vehicles of a cosmic *Geist*, at least in the non-demythologised interpretation, and thus the life of an individual, a group, nation or age has a meaning prior to it as a phase in the self-realisation of *Geist*. Likewise Marx appears to think of mankind as a collective entity and with a collective destiny, and as creating its own, and therefore internal, meaning through work and the transformation of Nature, culminating in the achevement of the classless society wherein the division of labour and the 'realm of necessity' is reduced to the absolute minimum. Again, the life of an individual, group, nation or age thereby has an extraneous meaning, task and destiny given to it, although nothing is given extraneously to mankind collectively. The danger, realised in totalitarian political movements, in such notions of life's meaning, which are also to be found in such 'science-myths' as those based on Evolution, is that the meaning of the individual's life becomes, not only extraneous, but extrinsic; not just something given to him from a source beyond him, but making him and his life of significance only in their effects upon something else – the self-realisation of *Geist*, the achievement of the classless society or the furtherance of Life. In such notions of life's meaning there is little meaning in the individual's life in itself nor in him. Therefore his leisure is of no importance either. It is his work, his function, living outside and beyond him which matters.

To be sure, those living in the final age, when the end imminent in the world is achieved, have value and meaning in themselves, and give extrinsic meaning to the lives of those who have gone before in so far as the latter have helped to bring in the final age. They, we might say, live in the leisured age when they attain and enjoy the fruits of what the past has achieved. Instead of leisure and mere work alternating in the individual's life, or being largely divided between separate classes, they are divided between, respectively, the final and all the preparatory ages. Hence the fanaticism when such world-views become translated into political action: only the End, or also its proximate stages, such as the Revolution and the dictatorship of the proletariat in Marxist theory, matters and has meaning, and to its achievement all else and everyone else becomes merely instrumental, usable or expendable. Hence what Dr Pieper called the 'state of total work' in which there is no leisure. And, when the final state is realised, what then is there for men to do save those things which the individualist interpretations envisage?

Consequently, we are brought back to the question of whether the mundane concerns mentioned in these discussions are enough to give life meaning or whether something more is needed, something which could be realised only beyond this life and this world. What, then, is 'the essence of things'? If it is itself a nothingness, a void of values, as much recent and contemporary philosophy holds (for example, Logical Positivism, Sartrean Existentialism and quite a lot of Analytic Philosophy), then we are left only with what we ourselves individually find to be of interest to us or by fiat make valuable and significant. And that, surely, is only a distraction, a *pis aller*, a filling of time, in default of a genuinely worthwhile end. A really worthwhle end would then be one set before us by something beyond ourselves, and perhaps beyond this world. It would also be an end which confers an intrinsic value upon the individual and to which he is not merely instrumental. And in that case, it seems, we can hardly stop short of finding in religious belief and worship the meaning of life and the proper content of leisure, as Dr Pieper argues.

It is enough for the present to have shown that leisure does raise the profound quesion of the meaning of life, of what would make life really worthwhile and whether or not it can be achieved in the world, and that therefore leisure also involves equally profound questions about the nature, scope and contents of philosophy in answering or being unable to answer those former questions.

Notes

1.   Josef Pieper, *Leisure: The Basis of Culture*, trans. A. Dru (London, 1952).
2.   Ibid., p. 103.
3.   Aristotle, *Nicomachean Ethics*, x 7.

4. Ibid.
5. See, for example, R. S. Peters, *Ethics and Education* (London, 1966); P. H. Hirst, *Knowledge and the Curriculum* (London, 1974); R. S. Downie, E. M. Loudfoot and E. Telfer, *Education and Personal Relations* (London, 1973); A. O'Hear, *Education, Society and Human Nature* (London, 1981).
6. One person who has addressed himself to this problem in several publications is Professor G. H. Bantock: his *Dilemmas of the Curriculum* (Oxford, 1980) summarises his views and refers to his other works.
7. Aristotle, *Nicomachean Ethics*, x 7.
8. Vladimir Soloviev, *Three Dialogues on War, Progress and the End of History: Including a Short Story of the Anti-Christ*, English trans. (London, 1915). Contrast the attitudes of the Politician, who sees the need for an army now in order to eliminate it in the future, with the General who says that, after God and Russia, he loves his work in the artillery the most.
9. Eric Gill, *A Holy Tradition of Working: Passages from the Writings of Eric Gill*, ed. B. Keeble (Cambridge, 1983).
10. Irving Babbitt, *Rousseau and Romanticism* (Cleveland, Ohio, 1955).
11. See the discussions of this theme by A. G. N. Flew in *Ethics*, vol. 73 (1963); K. Baier, *The Meaning of Life* (Canberra, 1957): K. Brittan, *Philosophy and the Meaning of Life* (Cambridge, Mass., 1970); P. Edwards, 'Life, Value and Meaning', in P. Edwards (ed.), *The Encyclopaedia of Philosophy* (London, 1967). The exception is R. Nozick, *Philosophical Explanations* (Oxford, 1981).
12. Baier, *The Meaning of Life*, p. 21.
13. Ibid., p. 27.
14. Edwards, 'Life, Value and Meaning', pp. 469–70.
15. Ibid., pp. 72–3.
16. Brittan, *Philosophy and the Meaning of Life*, p. 3.
17. Ibid., pp. 16–17.
18. Either implicitly or explicitly this notion is presented as the aim of education in the following, among other works: J. Wilson, *Introduction to Moral Education* (Harmondsworth, Middx, 1967), and *Education in Religion and the Emotions* (London, 1971); P. H. Hirst, *Moral Education in a Secular Society* (London, 1974); J. P. White, *Towards a Compulsory Curriculum* (London, 1973), and *The Aims of Education Restated* (London, 1982); R. Dearden, 'Autonomy as an Educational Ideal', in S. C. Brown (ed.), *Philosophers Discuss Education* (London, 1975); R. Barrow and R. Woods, *Introduction to Philosophy of Education* (London, 1982).
19. Nozick, *Philosophical Explanations*, pp. 579–609.
20. Ibid., p. 610.

3

Work, Leisure and Human Needs[1]

SEAN SAYERS

I

Issues of work and leisure are topical at the moment. We are living in a period of long-term, mass unemployment in much of the Western world. In Britain and some other parts of Europe it is approaching the scale of the 1930s.[2] In the aftermath of the Great Depression, and particularly in the period of postwar reconstruction, a consensus emerged committed to policies of full employment. This was to be achieved on the basis of steady economic growth, which was also to provide for a rising standard of living and a gradually increasing amount of leisure time.

In recent years, however, a growing chorus of voices has been questioning these ideas. Automation is bringing about the 'collapse of work'.[3] The traditional idea of full employment is no longer applicable: according to André Gorz, 'there can no longer be full time waged work for all'.[4]

These developments, it is said, herald the advent of the 'post industrial' age, which will involve profound changes in the places of work and leisure in human life: 'Socially useful labour . . . will cease to be anyone's exclusive or leading activity. Instead, people's major occupation may be one or a number of self-defined activities'.[5] Traditional attitudes are also changing. According to Gorz, a life centred on work is no longer either possible or desirable.

> An inversion of the scale of priorities, involving a subordination of socialised work . . . to activities constituting the sphere of individual autonomy, is underway. 'Real life' begins outside of work, and work itself has become a means towards the extension of the sphere of non-work, a temporary occupation by which individuals acquire the possibility of pursuing their main activities.[6]

Work, in the sense of socially necessary productive activity, cannot be a source of liberation or fulfilment: it is inevitably alienating. Work is a mere means to freedom, which can come only outside of work in free time. Work is unfreedom, leisure is liberation.

My aim in this paper is to question these views. My focus, however, will not be upon the economic and social prophesies about 'post-industrial' society (questionable as these are); but rather on the rethinking of moral attitudes to work and leisure which these are claimed to involve. For I shall argue that work is, and remains, a fundamental and central activity in human life. It is the basis upon which human nature develops and, potentially, at least, a fulfilling and liberating activity. In this context, I will then seek to clarify the role of leisure.

The Realm of Necessity

The idea that work can be a liberating activity is, of course, a central theme of Marx's philosophy, and of Hegel's too. As is often noted, however, Marx's pronouncements on the human meaning of work are not free of ambiguity.[7] In particular, in a well-known passage, Marx describes labour as activity in the realm of necessity, and he contrasts it with the true realm of freedom which 'begins only where labour which is determined by necessity . . . ceases'.[8] These phrases are often taken to imply that work, because it is a necessary activity, is therefore unfree and inescapably alienating; and they are accordingly seized upon by writers like Gorz in support of their case.[9]

My concern is not with Marx's ideas as such, and I have no wish to rescue him from the charge of ambiguity or contradiction here. Whatever Marx may have meant by these words, however, I do wish to argue that the necessity of work does not automatically imply its unfreedom.

That work is a human necessity is undeniable. We are creatures of need and we must work to satisfy our needs. From this evident truth it seems but a short step to the conclusion that work cannot be a liberating or fulfilling activity. According to Gorz, for example, 'work is an imposition, a heterodetermined, heteronomous activity. . . . Work is only a means of earning money and not an activity that is an end in itself. . . . Work is not freedom.'[10]

However, the necessity of work does not entail such conclusions. Quite the contrary. The feeling that one's work is useful and necessary is one of the major aspects of the fulfilment that work can bring. It can, to some extent, compensate for all sorts of other unsatisfactory and unpleasant features of work: long hours and low pay, difficulty and danger (as in the case of nurses and miners, for example). In saying this I must stress, I am not trying to suggest that some people will or should tolerate – still less enjoy – menial or degrading work simply because it is useful. This is what is implied by the familiar propaganda figure of the heroic worker happily and tirelessly toiling away at the most unappealing tasks simply for the good of society. My point is not so fanciful. Of course, there are useful jobs which are intrinsically unpleasant, and which peple shun despite their utility. It is quite possible to acknowledge this, however, without denying the point that I am making: namely, that the usefulness and necessity of work is often an important source of its satisfaction.

Conversely, where work is felt to be useless or unnecessary it becomes demoralising and even hateful. Such feelings should be familiar, for doubts about the need for one's work are a particular occupational hazard for philosophers and other academics, as well as people in advertising, the media, and others not directly engaged in the production of necessities. At the extreme, the lack of a useful social role is one of the greatest problems facing the unemployed; and retired people also suffer in this way. In the army, indeed, pointless exercises, like digging holes and filling them in again, are used as a cruel and unusual form of punishment.

These well-known facts about the psychology of work and the lack of it call in question the view that work, simply because it is necessary, is thereby experienced as a coercive imposition. Hegel and Marx recognise these aspects of work at a more theoretical level. Thus Hegel, in the 'Master-Slave' section of his *Phenomenology*, focuses upon the element of 'service' in the slave's labour; and in the *Philosophy of Right* he describes how work in its social form must be 'strictly adapted . . . to the pleasure [i.e. needs] of other workers'.[11] But so far from regarding these as purely negative and unfree features of work, he portrays them as essential to its self-formative and liberating character. Likewise, Marx. In unalienated labour, he writes, 'I have the *direct* enjoyment both of being conscious of having satisfied a *human* need by my work, that is, of having objectified man's *essential nature*, and of having thus created an object corresponding to the need of another *man's* essential nature.'[12]

Furthermore, work is necessary not only in that its purpose is to satisfy needs, but also in the activity it involves, in the *means* which it must use to this end. For the activity of work is, in large measure, set by its ends, and by the nature of the materials and the tools through which these ends are to be achieved. Thus, as Marx says, the worker's purpose 'determines the mode of his activity with the rigidity of a law and he must subordinate his will to it'.[13] This is also a Hegelian theme, as Lukács explains:

> In the Hegelian view of labour one of the crucial dialectical moments is that the active principle . . . must learn to respect reality just as it is. In the object of labour immutable laws are at work, labour can only be fruitful if these are known and recognised.[14]

Again, however, this does not entail that work in unfree. For it is by working on the world, by overcoming the obstacles that it presents and achieving our purposes in and through it, that we develop our capacities and powers and realise our freedom. Marx is particularly clear upon this point.

> Certainly, labour obtains its measure from the outside, through the aim to be attained and the obstacles to be overcome in attaining it. But . . . this overcoming of obstacles is in itself a liberating activity – and . . . further, the external aims become stripped of the semblance of merely external natural urgencies, and become posited as aims which the individual himself posits – hence as self-realisation, objectification of the subject, hence real freedom, whose action is, precisely, labour.[15]

Simone Weil makes this point in a powerful passage which is worth quoting at length.

> Perfect liberty cannot be conceived as consisting merely in the disappearance of . . . necessity . . . An existence from which the very notion of work had pretty well disappeared would be delivered over to the play of the passions and perhaps to madness; there is no self-mastery without discipline, and there is no other source of discipline for man than the effort demanded in overcoming external obstacles . . . Even the apparently freest forms of activity, science, art, sport, only possess value in so far as they imitate the accuracy, rigour, scrupulousness which characterise the performance of work, and even exaggerate them. Were it not for the model offered them unconsciously by the ploughman, the blacksmith, the sailor who work *comme il faut* – to use that admirably ambiguous expression –

they would sink into the purely arbitrary. The human body can in no case cease to depend on the mighty universe in which it is encased; even if man were to cease being subjected to material things and to his fellows by needs and dangers, he would only be more completely delivered into their hands by the emotions which would stir him continually to the depth of his soul, and against which no regular occupation would any longer protect him.[16]

In its modern forms, moreover, work is a social and co-operative activity. It is socially organised, socially co-ordinated, and governed by an increasingly complex and extensive division of labour. According to Gorz, this is a further respect in which work is inevitably an unfree and alienating activity. Work, he argues, has ceased to be an 'autonomous' activity in which the worker can exercise individual control and initiative in the production process. It has become a social process which imposes itself upon the individual worker in an external and coercive fashion.

Heteronomous work is the inevitable outcome of the socialisation of the productive process . . . The co-ordination of a vast number of specialised tasks demands pre-established rules and procedures, leaving no room for individual improvisation or inventiveness. The social productive system can only operate like a single gigantic machine, to which all separate activities must be subservient.[17]

It is true, of course, that the particular forms of the social organisation of modern industrial work are often incompatible with the development of individuality and freedom. They involve a division of labour which concentrates expertise and control in a select group of engineers and managers, and condemns the vast majority of workers to operations and tasks from which all aspects of skill and knowledge, and opportunities to exercise initiative and independence, have been deliberately and systematically eliminated. Moreover, it is by no means clear how far such forms of the division of labour can be altered within the context of modern industrial work. However, there is no need to resolve these issues in order to see the inadequacy of Gorz's position. For Gorz's argument involves an extreme individualism which would make short work of such questions. According to it, all forms of the division of labour (beyond the immediate household or small group level, at least), are incompatible with the development of individuality and freedom. Socially organised work – in itself and just as such – is alienating.

These views are untenable. Freedom and individuality are not innate human attributes which flourish naturally, and despite 'society' and its 'constraints'. On the contrary, human nature – including human freedom and individuality – is an historical product. It develops only in and through society. The activity of work, moreover, is crucial and central to this development. For, as Marx says, 'by . . . acting on the external world and changing it, [man] at the same time changes his own nature. He develops his slumbering powers and compels them to act in obedience to his sway'.[18]

This is a profound and fundamental insight. In work people develop and exercise their powers and capacities; and in doing so they develop and extend them. They thus acquire new skills and abilities; and these are the real basis, the real contents, of freedom and individuality. Moreover, as far back as we can trace them, these developments occur always within a social context.

Once more, these ideas have a Hegelian origin. 'The outstanding achievement' of Hegel's philosophy, writes Marx, is that he 'grasps the essence of labour and comprehends objective man . . . as the outcome of man's own labour. . . . [Man's] manifestation as a real species-being (i.e. as a human being) is only possible if he really brings out all his *species-powers* – something which in turn is only possible through the co-operative action of all mankind, only as the result of history'.[19] In short, the fact – and it is a fact – that social co-operation in work constrains and necessitates the actions of individuals, so far from ruling out freedom and autonomy, is the very condition for their development.

The Development of Needs

By working on the world we not only satisfy existing needs; we exercise and develop our skills and powers and create new needs. As Marx says, the production of new needs is 'the first historical act',[20] for it sets mankind on the path to historical development. The 'realm of necessity', the sphere of needs, expands; but so, too, do our productive powers, our ability to satisfy them. Capitalism and modern industry, in particular, promote a gigantic increase in production and a corresponding growth of needs.

There are two different ways of reacting to these developments. On the one hand, with Rousseau, the growth of human needs may be looked upon as an essentially negative and undesirable phenomenon. Mankind, he argues, is at its freest and happiest in the early stages of its historical development, when needs are minimal. With social development, our needs expand more rapidly than our ability to satisfy them. The growth of needs is thus an evil – a cause of suffering, a sign of want and lack within us. The greater our needs, the weaker and more dependent, the more enslaved and unfree, we become. The sphere of needs constitutes an ever increasing realm of unfreedom.[21]

Such a picture of human need also underlies the position of Gorz and other 'post industrial' writers; and their social recipes follow from this. Modern industry has created a whole array of 'false' needs for its products. The way to freedom and happiness is not through an increase in production and an expansion of needs. Quite the reverse, Gorz insists, we should not only 'work fewer hours', but also 'consume less and have fewer needs': 'The voluntary, collective limitation of the sphere of necessity is the . . . only way to guarantee an extension of the sphere of autonomy [i.e., freedom].'[22]

Hegel and Marx, as we have just seen, have a quite different view. They regard the growth of human needs as an essential aspect of the development of human nature. In general, it is beneficial and positive – the pathway to human freedom. For human nature is social and historical in character. Human nature – human needs and human freedom – grows and develops historically. As regards needs, what are luxuries for one generation become necessities for the next. And we now take for granted many things which would have been beyond the power of earlier generations even to conceive.

This is not to deny that 'false needs' are engendered in modern society. However, it is to insist that the distinction between 'true' and 'false' needs must always be conceived in historical and relative terms. And it does involve rejecting the romantic attempt to circumscribe a fixed sphere of 'natural' or 'true' needs, and condemn as harmful and corrupting all developments of human nature beyond this basic level.

This, at least, is Hegel's view. Thus he responds to the Rousseauian position by first insisting, as I have, upon 'the moment of liberation intrinsic to work'; and secondly by arguing that the simple and primitive life of the 'state of nature' is the very opposite of genuine freedom. Rather it is an animal-like and *merely* natural condition: 'To be confined to mere physical needs as such and their direct satisfaction would simply be the condition in which the mental is plunged in the natural and so would be one of savagery and unfreedom.'[23]

Such talk of 'savagery' may upset modern sensibilities, but this should not be allowed to obscure the point that Hegel is making. It is shared in its essentials by Marx as well. For Marx, needs are not a purely negative feature of human life, they are not something merely suffered. Springborg has an inkling of this when she observes that 'it is a curiosity of Marx's theory of human nature that there is a close association between the concepts of needs and powers'.[24] However, this association is much more that a mere 'curiosity'. It is a central feature of Marx's theory. Needs are the negative side of what exists in a positive form as human powers and capacities. As our powers and capacities develop, so new needs emerge; and, in turn, the growth of new needs is the spur to the development of new powers and capacities. Needs and powers are two different, negative and positive, sides of the same process – the growth of human nature. Márkus makes this crucial point when he writes that, for Marx,

> man's nature is a 'totality of needs and drives',[25] and in this living unity of the real personality 'passive' wants and 'active' capacities reciprocally presuppose each other and mutually transform into each other. . . . For man, on the one hand, is an *active* being, i.e. he can satisfy his wants only by developing and exercising his abilities and, on the other hand, the once-formed capability demands some scope for itself, i.e. it appears as a specific need for activity.[26]

Moreover, the development of human nature does not remain confined to the sphere of purely material needs and capacities. For the growth of material needs and activities leads to the emergence and development of 'higher', mental and cultural, needs and abilities, and hence to the development of the sphere of autonomy and freedom.

In this way, the development of needs, so far from corrupting and enslaving mankind, is the essential basis for human liberation. For real freedom is a positive and not a merely negative phenomenon. It is not the mere antithesis of necessity. It is attained not through a restriction of needs or a limitation of the realm of necessity, as writers like Gorz maintain. It requires, rather, the fullest possible extension and expansion of this sphere and hence of human nature, involving, in Marx's words, 'the universality of individual needs, capacities, pleasures, productive forces, etc. . . . The full development of human mastery over the forces of nature, those of so-called nature as well as humanity's own nature. The absolute working out of his creative potentialities.'[27]

A Protestant Ethic?

In short, work is, in various ways, a necessary activity; but it is not thereby inevitably alienating and unfree. On the contrary, its very necessity is at the basis of its potentially liberating character. That is what I have been arguing. In doing so, I am bound to be accused of putting forward a version of the 'Protestant work ethic'. It is true, no doubt, that the views I have been defending constitute a 'work ethic', for they give work a central place in human life. However, it is important to see that this work ethic differs fundamentally from the traditional Protestant version.

Protestantism characteristically involves what Weber calls an 'ascetic' morality.[28] At the same time as it extols work as the God-given duty and 'calling' of mankind, it adopts a forbidding attitude towards leisure, and particularly the pleasures of consumption and the satisfaction of needs, which it looks upon as mere 'idleness' and 'indulgence'. In this way, the Protestant ethic opposes work to leisure, production to consumption, activity to idleness, and values the one to the exclusion of the other.

It is evident that a strong puritanical streak also runs through some versions of socialist morality. For example, leisure and pleasure have no place in the life of the heroic, Stakhanovite worker of Soviet propaganda, whose sole satisfaction seems to consist in the performance of socially useful labour. The view that I am defending is quite different from this. For there is nothing puritanical about the Marxist account of human nature, nor about the idea of socialism which follows from it. On the contrary, as we have seen, Marx's philosophy involves a vision of the full development of human nature – of our 'needs, capacities, pleasures, productive forces, etc.'. The expansion of needs and their *enjoyment* is as much a part of this picture as the growth of production. Indeed, it is rather Gorz and others who criticise 'consumer society' in a romantic fashion, who can rightly be charged with asceticism and puritanism. For they want to limit the development of our needs and constrict the pleasures of consumption.[29]

II

The Need for Leisure

To argue that work is a central and potentially satisfying activity is not to say that it is, or ever could be, the *sole* source of fulfilment or self-development. It is clear that we cannot be active, let alone at work, all the time. The question which then arises is: what is the place of non-work, of leisure, in human life?

In the first place, apart from activity, we also need inactivity: rest and sleep. These are natural, physical and bodily needs; even though the specific amount of rest and sleep required shows considerable historical, social and individual variation. There are good grounds for thinking that the need for rest is connected with the demands of work. When people are made unemployed they tend to sleep more than when they were in work. Moreover, people in industrial societies tend to be more energetic and active, they rest and sleep considerably less than people from pre-industrial societies.[30] This is a theme in Mrs Gaskell's *North and South* (written 1854–5), where we see the northern industrial town of 'Milton' through the eyes of the Hales, newly arrived from the still agrarian south of England: 'After a quiet life in a country parsonage for more than twenty years there was something dazzling to Mr Hale in the energy which conquered immense difficulties with ease; the power of the machinery of Milton, the power of the men of Milton, impressed him with a sense of grandeur.'[31]

Secondly, people in modern society need not only rest but also activities and satisfactions outside work. They need leisure. It is worth noting that Marx was not properly aware of this in his earliest works, where he tends to focus exclusively on the division of *labour* and its overcoming. In *The German Ideology*, for example, he imagines a society in which we could 'hunt in the morning, fish in the afternoon, breed cattle in the evening, criticise after dinner'.[32] This suggests that all activities apart from rest (but including 'criticism') can be considered under the heading of 'labour', as aspects of the division of labour. In his later works, however, he comes to recognise the need for free, non-work time, 'which is both idle time and time for higher activities'.[33]

When Gorz and other advocates of 'post industrial' society speak of leisure replacing work as central in people's lives, it is clear that they do not mean mere rest and sleep. Gorz talks of a sphere of 'autonomous activity' which, he insists, 'is not based upon a mere desire to consume, not solely upon relaxation. . . . It is based, more profoundly, upon activities unrelated to any economic goal which are an end in themselves'[34] – hobbies and craft work, sports and recreation, cultural, artistic and social activities. The characteristic feature of leisure, as thus conceived, is that it is not work, not in 'the realm of necessity', not undertaken from economic compulsion but as an end in itself.

The Growth of Leisure

Unlike rest and sleep, however, such activity is not a natural need and not a natural part of human life. On the contrary, it is an historically developed sphere of activity. It is important to stress this, for there is a strong tendency in writers like Gorz to look back nostalgically to the pre-industrial period and portray it as a time of more 'natural' attitudes to work and leisure. Thus, 'in all pre-capitalist societies', according to Gorz, leisure activities

> were embedded into productive work. Work was given its rhythm by festivals and celebrations, with their songs and dances; the tools were beautifully decorated. . . . There was . . . a genuine 'popular art' which integrated work and life to create a way of living that had meaning and value. . . . There was no separation between work, culture and life.[35]

It is true that in the earliest communal forms of society, based on hunting and gathering, it is not possible to distinguish clearly between work and leisure, either in society as a whole or in the lives of individuals. Virtually all members of the community (apart from young children) participate in the necessary labour of society (though normally subject to a division of labour by sex), and there is little provision for the support of unproductive members: infanticide is common and senilicide is sometimes also practised.[36] Work and what, by modern standards, would be regarded as 'leisure' are intermingled in the course of daily life. On a Tikopian working party, writes Firth, 'the whole atmosphere is one of labour diversified by recreation at will'.[37] However, as Sahlins reminds us,

> the periodic deflection from 'work' to 'ritual' by peoples such as the Tikopians . . . must be made without prejudice, for their linguistic categories know no such distinction, but conceive both activities sufficiently serious as to merit a common term . . . the 'work of the Gods'.[38]

The Yir Yiront, an Australian Aboriginal group, do not even draw a distinction between 'work' and 'play'.

In such societies, needs are few, life is simple and work leisurely by modern standards, not only in its pace and rhythms, but also in its duration. As Sahlins shows, a good case can be made that hunters and gatherers work less than we do; and, rather than a continual travail, the food quest is intermittent, leisure abundant, and there is a greater amount of sleep in the daytime per capita per year than in any other condition of society.[39]

If the mere absence of work is sufficient to constitute leisure, we should have to look backwards to these societies for our models of the 'leisure society'. But this would be a mistake. For if their work is leisurely, it is also the case that their 'leisure' is necessary. Indeed, to talk of 'leisure' in this context is problematic: for much of the non-work activity of such peoples is not 'free' or 'autonomous', not undertaken as an end in itself. The arts and crafts, the rituals and ceremonies, of such societies form an essential aspect of the necessary labour of subsistence. As Sahlins says,

> it would be insufficient simply to suppose that production is . . . subject to arbitrary interference . . . by other obligations, themselves 'non-economic'. . . . These other claims – of ceremony, diversion, sociability and repose – are only the complement or, if you will, the superstructural counterpart of a dynamic proper to the economy.[40]

The growth of a sphere of leisure, distinct from work, goes together with the emergence of classes and groups exempt from necessary work. The economic basis of this development is the distinction between necessary and surplus labour. Necessary labour is the work needed to reproduce the working portion of society at its given, historically developed, level of subsistence; while surplus labour is production above and beyond this, which creates the basis for a privileged group of non-workers.[41] So, too, it creates the basis upon which 'higher' leisure activities have developed.

> The labour of the mass has [been] . . . the condition for the development of general wealth, just as the non-labour of the few [has been the condition] for the development of the general powers of the human mind.[42]

Capitalism and Modern Leisure

Capitalism, in particular, is ruthlessly geared towards the expansion of surplus labour. In the first stages of industrialism, this was achieved partly by lengthening the working day and enforcing more regular habits of work. The separation of work and non-work time was completed in this period[43]; though it would be wrong to talk of 'leisure' in this context, since the work day was so extended that workers had insufficient time even for adequate rest and recuperation. Subsequently, however, the major part of the expansion of surplus labour has been achieved by increasing the efficiency and productivity of labour. The continual drive to improve productivity, through the introduction of new machinery is, indeed, a characteristic feature of capitalist development: 'the bourgeoisie cannot exist without constantly revolutionising the instruments of production'.[44]

It is all too easy to think that greater production must involve more hours of work; and conversely, that a reduction in work must entail producing and consuming less. Gorz, for one, tends to make these equations. As we have seen, he thinks that we should both 'work fewer hours' and 'consume less', and he often writes as if the two went hand in hand. However, one of the revolutionary effects of modern industry has been to break this connection: 'To the degree that large industry develops, the creation of real wealth comes to depend less on labour time and on the amount of labour employed than on the power of the agencies set in motion during labour time.'[45]

The gigantic increase in production that has been achieved during the last 150 years has provided the basis *both* for a steadily rising standard of living and growth of needs among the working population as a whole; *and*, at the same time, for a gradual decrease in work hours – in the United States, for example, from an average of about 70 hours per week in 1850, to 41.5 hours in 1956.[46] The resulting free time, coupled with the growing needs and capacities of working people, has created the basis for the modern phenomenon of mass leisure. Leisure in its modern sense – as a sphere of positive non-work activity enjoyed by the mass of working people – is thus a modern phenomenon and a product of modern industry. Crucial to its development is not only the reduction in hours of work but also the development of needs and capacities for leisure activities. It is these which give modern leisure its distinctive character, and make it not simply a time of passivity and idleness, but a sphere of activity and creativity.

These leisure activities include what Gorz calls 'autonomous creative activities' – gardening, do-it-yourself and craftwork, etc. No doubt, working people were productively active in such ways long before the modern period.[47] However, except in situations of unemployment, these activities now have the character of leisure activities: they are outside the sphere of economic necessity and engaged in primarily for the pleasure of the activity itself (though often, to be sure, their utility is a part of the pleasure).[48]

At the same time, education has been extended. The rise of the mass media – TV, newspapers, popular literature and music – has brought about a great increase in people's cultural experience. It is common to decry the debasing effects of these developments on the contents of popular culture; but at the same time the mass media have helped to inform and educate, widen horizons and introduce an unprecedented range of art and culture into people's lives. Recreation and sports are now widespread. Social life has been enhanced, with the growth of pubs, clubs and restraurants. Opportunities for holidays and travel have extended.[49]

I stress these developments not to endorse uncritically the particular forms that modern leisure takes, but rather to emphasise the profound changes which have occurred in the last 100 years in patterns of non-work activity. Through a reduction in work hours from the extreme lengths reached in the early years of the nineteenth century was a necessary condition for these changes, none would have happened through a reduction of work time alone. All have equally required the growth needs and capacities, institutions and facilities, of one sort or another.

All, moreover, involve people as consumers to a greater or lesser extent; and developing consumer needs has become an important and quite deliberate part of the work of capitalist industry. In this respect, its characteristic strategy and attitudes have changed profoundly. In the early stages of industrialism, a puritanical attitude to both consumption and leisure prevailed. The churches and industry together campaigned against the pleasures and recreations of the working class. They aimed to curb drinking, both on and off the job; and they sought to limit the fairs, festivals and holidays which were the main popular forms of leisure and enjoyment.[50]

Nowadays, by contrast, we are encouraged to consume, to develop and indulge our pleasures and enjoyments. Capitalism is anything but puritanical in its attitude to leisure. It is rather Gorz, and others like him who hanker after the plain and simple life, who are the new puritans. For they want an increase in leisure without the expansion of consumer needs and capacities for activity and enjoyment which economic development brings. Marx's idea was different. There is nothing puritanical about it. He welcomed the massive growth of production brought about by capitalism as one of its 'civilising aspects',[51] not only because it permits an expansion of leisure time, but also because it creates the needs and capacities required to make this time truly a 'realm of freedom'.

> Real economy – saving – consists of the saving of labour time . . . but this saving [is] identical with [the] development of the productive force[s]. Hence in no way [is it] *abstinence from consumption*, but rather the development of power, of capabilities of production, and hence both of the capability as well as the means of consumption.[52]

The Relation of Work and Leisure

Leisure is a modern phenomenon which has come to occupy an increasingly important place in life. According to Gorz, indeed, the 'sphere of autonomy' is now our main priority, and work is regarded simply as a means to it. But this, I now want to suggest, is a one-sided way of interpreting these developments. Certainly, economic development has created free time – Gorz is right about that. It has also led to the growth of the needs and capacities required for the active enjoyment of it. These are the large-scale trends of the last 150 years, and there is every reason to expect that they will continue. However, although it is true that leisure plays an increasing role in people's lives, there are grounds to be sceptical of the view that it has replaced work as the central human priority and goal.

Gorz would have us bid 'farewell to the working class' and to Marxism, while he presents his own views as if they were the latest thing in 'post-industrial' thought. But there is nothing novel, let alone 'post-industrial', about the idea that work is a curse and leisure the main good. Quite the contrary. In most class societies up until now there has been a privileged leisure class, which has monopolised education and culture, and embodied the ideals of the highest and most worthy forms of life (artist, scientist, statesman, warrior, and so on). A notable feature of the modern period, however, is that alongside the rise of mass leisure, there has been a significant decline of the purely leisured class of the idle rich. According to Henri Lefebvre, 'a man of my age has with his own eyes seen, between 1880 and 1940, the final fall of the man who does nothing, does no work, the *"rentier-idler"* '.[53] As the idle rich decline, so too does the aristocratic, non-work ethic. Wealthy men – and increasingly women, too – more and more feel obliged to engage in some sort of work-like activity.

Even the Royal Family are expected to 'work' for their (very considerable) income, and are criticised when it is felt that they are not performing a sufficient number of public functions. Contrary to what Gorz and other prophets of 'post-industrial' society suggest, the view that the ideal life is one of pure leisure is ceasing to have application or real basis in the modern world.

Rather, it is felt increasingly that leisure has value only in the context of work, as a complement to work. Whereas when it is divorced from work, and made an exclusive activity, it loses its value. The most dramatic demonstration of this is the experience of unemployment. By Gorz's standards, unemployment, as a total 'liberation from work', should constitute the complete realisation of leisure, autonomy and freedom. But it would be grotesque to think of unemployment in these terms. For it is a quite different phenomenon to leisure or freedom, and not just because of the economic hardship it so often involves.[54]

Leisure activities, like reading, gardening, knitting, watching TV or meeting friends in the pub, are pleasurable and fulfilling in the context of a life of work; but on their own, and outside that context, they are not capable of providing a satisfactory filling for life. What may be enjoyable and rewarding as a hobby or spare time activity is insufficient as the central activity of life. For such pursuits have value primarily in contrast to work – and precisely because they are not work, not necessary activities, but engaged in simply for the pleasure they bring.

One's own pleasure is not a sufficient end or purpose in life. People – virtually all people – want and need something more than this. They want and need activity which achieves something in the public realm and which contributes usefully to society. In short, they want work as well as leisure. By way of illustration, I will mention a conversation I had recently on these topics with an acquaintance. He has a son in his mid-twenties. The son had been to college, but his studies had not engaged his interests and he had not done well. After college he did not get a job. He had a talent for music – he played the drums – but he was repelled by the commercialism of the world of professional music, and felt he would have to make too many compromises to make a career in it. At present he is living on social security, slowly fixing up a derelict house, and playing music with his friends. He didn't want a job. He was happy, his father told me, and presented the story as a refutation of the argument I have been defending.

Such stories are now quite common, at least among a particular group of people in the Western world. Gorz's philosophy, indeed, generalises them and seeks to justify, in theoretical terms, the attitude to work and leisure that they illustrate. To what extent do they cast doubt upon the argument I have been presenting? The young man in question is evidently an educated and relatively privileged person, in a better position than many unemployed people. That is not without significance. One could quote a good number of less happy stories of unemployment. But leaving that point aside and staying with this story, the question still arises: is this an ideal or even a satisfactory life?

Music as a hobby is one thing. In that case it is a complement to work and a relaxation from it: something that is pursued for pleasure, self-expression and self-cultivation; with no more asked of it than that. But if it is to be the central activity of one's life, then it takes on a different character and one is likely to put different demands on it. For few people find mere self-cultivation a sufficient end in life; nor is the work of the artist usually a matter of mere self-expression. The young man that I have just mentioned is not necessarily a refutation of this. For it is one thing to 'drop out' when one is young, but the evidence suggests that few remain content with such a life as they grow older.[55]

Of course, there are exceptions to this generalisation. Some artists pursue their art purely out of a driving inner and purely personal need for self-expression[56] but they are rare. More often, the artist wants to create something which satisfies not just his *own* inner needs, but also the needs of *others*.[57] He wants to *communicate*. He wants his work to find an audience and be appreciated. He is engaged in a creative, a productive activity, which, like all productive activities, is ultimately completed and brought to consummation only in consumption. Marx makes this point in general terms when he writes,

> a product becomes a real product only by being consumed. For example, a garment becomes a real garment only by being worn; a house where no one lives is in fact not a real house; thus the product, unlike a mere natural object, proves itself to be, *becomes*, a product only through consumption.[58]

When it has this communicative character, art can be among the highest activities. However, it also then has the character of a productive activity. On the other hand, if its only purpose is individual pleasure and self-cultivation, then it is reduced to the level of a mere hobby and pastime, which, although it may be valuable and rewarding in the context of a life of work, it is not sufficient in itself.

In the allegory of the Cave in the *Republic*, Plato describes how the philosopher, once he has struggled out of the Cave – once he has reached the sunlight and achieved a knowledge of the Form of the Good – must return into the darkness of the Cave and impart his knowledge to the prisoners still confined there. Plato argues that the philosopher must do this in the social interest.[59] However, what I am suggesting here is that it is equally in the philosopher's *own* interest to make this return journey. For philosophy, like art, music and other creative activities, is realised most fully when it meets *social* and not merely individual needs. In the context of a life productive in other areas, one may not demand or even wish so much from philosophy. But if it is the central activity of one's life then one surely will. For productive activity – activity which meets needs and is in the sphere of necessity – is fundamental to human fulfilment.

I have been criticising the ideas of Gorz and other advocates of 'post-industrial' society. Against them, I have argued that work is and remains the central activity of human life. I am well aware that for many people today these ideas will be of little comfort. A large number of people are currently unemployed or facing the prospect of unemployment. This is a human tragedy: that is the implication of what I am saying. I have offered no practical solutions or remedies. However, I write with the conviction that it is better to recognise these problems for what they are than to hold out the false hope that the advent of 'post-industrial' society will somehow render unemployment acceptable as a way of life.

Notes

1. An earlier version of this paper appeared originally in *Thesis Eleven*, no. 14 (1986) pp. 79–96. It is reprinted here with permission of the editors. I am grateful to George Márkus for helpful comments on an earlier draft.
2. 'With three and a quarter million unemployed – 14% of the workforce – in the autumn of 1982, Britain has reached the unemployment level that was the annual average during the interwar Depression' (K. Kumar, 'Unemployment as a Problem in the Development of Industrial Societies: the English Experience', *Sociological Review*, vol. 32 (1984) p. 233. In November 1985 the unemployment rate in Britain was 13.8 per cent.
3. C. Jenkins and B. Sherman, *The Collapse of Work* (London, 1979).
4. A. Gorz, *Paths to Paradise* (London, 1985) p. 34.
5. A. Gorz, *Farewell to the Working Class* (London, 1982) p. 3.
6. Ibid., p. 81.
7. See, for example, H. Arendt, *The Human Condition* (Chicago, 1958)

pp. 105–15; R. N. Berki, 'On the Nature and Origins of Marx's Concept of Labour', *Political Theory*, vol. 7 (1979) pp. 35–56.

8. K. Marx, *Capital*, vol. III (Moscow, 1971) p. 820.
9. Gorz, *Farewell to the Working Class*, pp. 95ff; Gorz, *Paths to Paradise*, pp. 59ff.
10. Gorz, *Farewell to the Working Class*, pp. 1–2.
11. G. W. F. Hegel, *The Philosophy of Right*, trans. T. M. Knox (Oxford, 1942) p. 129 (§197).
12. K. Marx, 'Comments on James Mill', *Élémens d'économie politique*', in K. Marx and F. Engels, *Collected Works*, vol. 3 (London, 1975) pp. 227–8.
13. Marx, *Capital*, vol. I (Moscow, 1961) p. 178. I have modified the translation in line with the Penguin edition (1978) p. 284.
14. G. Lukács, *The Young Hegel* (London, 1975) pp. 324–5. Cf. Bacon's dictum, 'nature [cannot] be commanded except by being obeyed' (F. Bacon, *New Organon* (Indianapolis, 1960) p. 29.
15. K. Marx, *Grundrisse* (Harmondsworth, Middx, 1973) p. 611.
16. S. Weil, *Oppression and Liberty* (London, 1958) pp. 84–5. It should be noted that Simone Weil here portrays the effects of work as primarily *negative* in character, as a matter of 'self discipline'; whereas Marx, as we shall see, is more conscious of the positive, self-developing aspects of labour.
17. Gorz, *Paths to Paradise*, pp. 50–1.
18. Marx, *Capital*, vol. I, p. 177.
19. K. Marx, 'Economic and Philosophic Manuscripts of 1844', in Marx and Engels, *Collected Works*, vol. 3.
20. K. Marx and F. Engels, *The German Ideology*, Part I, ed. C. J. Arthur (New York, 1978) p. 49.
21. J. J. Rousseau, *A Discourse on Inequality*, ed. M. Cranston (Harmondsworth, Middx, 1984).
22. Gorz, *Farewell to the Working Class*, pp. 122, 124.
23. Hegel, *The Philosophy of Right*, p. 128 (§194).
24. P. Springborg, *The Problem of Human Needs and the Critique of Civilization* (London, 1981) p. 98.
25. Marx, *Grundrisse*, p. 245.
26. G. Márkus, *Marxism and Anthropology* (Assen, 1978) pp. 63–4.
27. Marx, *Grundrisse*, p. 488.
28. M. Weber, *The Protestant Ethic and the Spirit of Capitalism*, trans. T. Parsons (New York, 1958).
29. See also M. Ignatieff, *The Needs of Strangers* (London, 1984) ch. 4.
30. S. Sayers, 'The Need to Work', *Radical Philosophy*, vol. 46 (1987) pp. 17–26.
31. E. Gaskell, *North and South* (Harmondsworth, Middx, 1970) p. 108.
32. Marx and Engels, *The German Ideology*, p. 53.
33. Marx, *Grundrisse*, p. 712.
34. Gorz, *Farewell to the Working Class*, p. 80.
35. Gorz, *Paths to Paradise*, pp. 48–9.
36. M. Sahlins, *Stone Age Economics* (London, 1974) p. 34.
37. Quoted ibid., p. 57.

38. Ibid., p. 64.
39. Ibid., p. 14.
40. Ibid., p. 65.
41. 'The creation of surplus labour on one side corresponds to the creation of minus-labour, relative idleness (or *non-productive* labour at best) on the other' (Marx, *Grundrisse*, p. 401n).
42. Ibid., p. 705.
43. For a very interesting account of this development see E. P. Thompson, 'Time, Work-discipline and Industrial Capitalism', *Past and Present*, vol. 38 (1967) pp. 56–97.
44. Marx and Engels, *The Communist Manifesto*, in *Selected Works*, vol. ı p. 36.
45. Marx, *Grundrisse*, p. 704.
46. J. S. Zeisel, 'The Workweek in American Industry, 1850–1956', in E. Larrabee and R. Meyersohn (eds), *Mass Leisure* (Glencoe, Ill., 1958) pp. 145–53.
47. R. E. Pahl, *Divisions of Labour* (London, 1984).
48. 'Hunting and fishing, the most important employments of mankind in the rude state of society, become in its most advanced state their most agreeable amusements, and they pursue for pleasure what they once followed from necessity' (A. Smith, *Wealth of Nations*, quoted in U. Pagano, *Work and Welfare in Economic Theory* (London, 1985) p. 21).
49. A good account of the development of modern leisure is given in J. Dumazedier, *Towards a Society of Leisure* (New York, 1967) chs 1–2.
50. S. Pollard, *The Genesis of Modern Management* (London, 1965) ch. 5; Thompson, 'Time, Work-discipline and Industrial Capitalism'.
51. Marx, *Capital*, vol. ııı, p. 819.
52. Marx, *Grundrisse*, p. 711.
53. Quoted in Dumazedier, *Towards a Society of Leisure*, p. 35.
54. M. Jahoda makes this point well in 'The Impact of Unemployment in the 1930s and the 1970s', *Bulletin of the British Psychological Society*, vol. 30 (1979) pp. 309–14; see also M. Jahoda, *Employment and Unemployment* (Cambridge, 1982).
55. Evidence on this point is usefully summarised and discussed in the US Department of Health, Education and Welfare Report, *Work in America* (Cambridge, Mass., 1973).
56. The central character in Somerset Maugham, *The Moon and Sixpence* comes to mind. Maugham is supposed to have based him on Gauguin.
57. Objective and external demands are sometimes a necessary stimulus to creative activity. Writers often feel that they need a deadline – an external and even coercive demand – to unleash their pens.
58. Marx, *Grundrisse*, p. 91.
59. Plato, *The Republic*, trans. H. D. P. Lee (Harmondsworth, Middx, 1955) pp. 278–86 (514A–521B).

4

Lived Time, Leisure and Retirement

MAURICE ROCHE

INTRODUCTION

Before I turn to lived time and the main themes of the paper I will flag some general assumptions about philosophy or theory which are likely, and rightly, to be suspected to be guiding my discussion from off-stage. They are modern humanistic and neo-classical assumptions, responsive to the spirit rather than the letter of Greek philosophy and its assumptions about the methods and purposes and the social role and content of theorising.[1] The assumptions hold for theorising about any topic but perhaps particularly about leisure, given that this form of experience was intimately connected with each of the aspects of Greek philosophy mentioned.[2] Whether in the form of leisure or, along the lines suggested in this paper, in the form of leisureliness, some such concept remains an important element in a realistic characterisation of philosophy's method, purpose and condition – the practice of contemplation and reflection, of conversation, criticism and education seem incomprehensible to me without such a recognition of leisure's significance.

However, that is another argument (and another paper). For the moment, the main assumption about theorising I wish to register is as follows. Theorising can only be carried on in a serious and consistent way (rather than in a whimsical and arbitrary way) in the form of a dialogue with versions of the way the world (including human beings): (i) is, (ii) ought to be, (iii) was, and (iv) can be. These versions can be generated 'in-house' as they were, for example, within Greek philosophy, or they can be encountered 'externally'; for example, in the movements of ideology and the developments of sciences operating in philosophy's social context. But there must be grist to theory's mill, and nutritional purpose to the mill's grinding. Hence there is a need to bring description, speculation and evaluation about

54

the world in a substantial and clear-headed way into the sphere of discussions which have a philosophical purpose, if only as a preparation of some of the resources necessary for adequate theoretical inquiry. It is along these lines that I would account for the descriptive, evaluative and hence arguably pre-philosophical character of much of the discussion that follows in the paper.

A 'philosophy of leisure', therefore, needs to exist as a dialogue with and a critical enrichment of the range of versions of what leisure was and is in modern social life (from the personal to the historiographical and social scientific), and with the range of versions of what it ought to be and can be (from the ideological to the medical, from state policy to futurology). It goes without saying that we will necessarily be able only to dip into some of this range of versions of leisure in this paper. That fact circumscribes the reasonable ambitions of the discussion. So the paper aims to be a preliminary orientation to leisure as a phenomenon in our world, and will do little more, but not less, than touch on and take *some* account of such issues as definitions of what leisure is; evaluations of whether 'it' is good or bad (for example, healthy or unhealthy) for people; and speculations about how best to model and anticipate the growth of 'it' that our post-industrial future promises or threatens. The paper focuses, on the one hand, on the general topic of *lived time* in order to contribute to thinking about the former two issues (definition and evaluation) and, on the other hand, on the specific topic of *retirement* in order to both illustrate the lived time discussion and also to contribute to thinking about the latter issue (leisure in our post-industrial future).[3]

The discussion is divided into three stages and the route is as follows. In section I the definition of leisure is considered, along with the importance to any such definition of notions of work and time. That the three notions are bound together in some less than happy and holy marriage has long been recognised, not least by Sebastian de Grazia who a generation ago helped to found and to give academic credibility to leisure studies research in his thoughtful and classically inspired study.[4] This section begins a discussion with some of de Grazia's views taken together with the comparable views of Geoffrey Godbey which lead to the need to provide some account of the experience of time. Section II then offers a schematic outline of lived time and of both unhealthy and negatively valued temporal experiences, 'time-stress', and also healthy and positively valued temporality, 'leisureliness'. These notions, particularly time-stress are illustrated with reference to the study of employment and unemployment. Section III offers some descriptions of the nature of retirement experience with a view to illustrating the 'leisureliness' aspect of the lived time analysis. It is hoped that this discussion will also suggest the heuristic significance of the notion for further research, both of a descriptive (ethnographic, phenomenological) and also of a speculative (sociological, futurological) kind.

It is the pursuit of these kinds of research – only briefly indicated in this paper – that will, I believe, provide the grist to the theorist's mill which a worthwhile 'philosophy of leisure' needs. Given its intentionally programmatic character the paper does not aim to achieve decisive conclusions about lived time and leisure. Rather it aims to achieve a preliminary and provisional understanding of their nature and relationship, and also of the material they offer and the agenda they imply for further theoretical inquiry and philosophical dialogue.

I *OF TIME, WORK AND LEISURE* (REVISITED)

What is leisure? How is it normally understood? As de Grazia made clear, leisure is incomprehensible by itself and only properly comprehended if its relations with time and work are also understood. I will return to de Grazia's views below. First let us begin with the commonsensical and sociological conception of leisure, of the 'natural attitude' to leisure. Leisure in modern industrial societies has come to be understood as whatever it is that people do in time periods in which they are not working in employment. Since industrialisation and the organisation, measurement and evaluation of work in terms of money and clocktime, leisure has come to be associated with these daily, weekly and annual periods of time in which one is not working.[5] So leisure is primarily understood, both by ordinary people and also by the various sorts of social scientists and leisure researchers who study them, in terms of a concept of time which provides both for a division of 'its' duration into measurable periods, blocks or zones, and also for an understanding of these zones as either 'free' or 'unfree' depending on whether paid employment is undertaken in them or not. Leisure then, is whatever is done in 'free time'. Despite a growing sophistication about the analysis of free and unfree time/time-zones, most studies in this field still tend to replicate this basic underlying natural attitude to leisure and this connection between leisure and assumptions about the nature of time and its significance in people's experience.[7] Leisure activities are defined by comparison with employment activities, and leisure time is defined by comparison with, and in opposition to, time in employment. A corollary of this is the implication that leisure-time increases as employment time decreases.

In recent history, however, changes in the structure of modern economies and in the nature of employment have rendered ambiguous and paradoxical the experience of time and leisure in the two increasingly important statuses outside of employment: unemployment and retirement.[8] These statuses are rarely voluntarily chosen, usually involve an income loss and can involve some experiences of psychological deprivation. None the less they also appear to luxuriate in 'free time' and thus in time for leisure. But appearances can be deceptive, for those who are 'rich' in time can also be relatively unhappy, particularly if they are also poor. My view is that there is something wrong with the 'natural attitude' conception of leisure and its associated conception of time if it leads to such paradoxes as this.

One of my tasks in this paper will be to try to proceed beyond the natural attitude conception, and to try to formulate a more viable and adequate conception of the relation between leisure and time. To help think through the problem it is worth recalling two important, useful and comparable critiques of the experience and concept of leisure in modern industrial societies: those of de Grazia and Godbey. In brief, their negative and positive views about leisure are as follows. Directing his critique at the modern notion that leisure is defined in terms of free time, de Grazia comments:

> whatever free time we have is unfree from the start. . . . That we oppose it to work really indicates that we still regard work as the dominant obligation. Any time after it is finished is 'free', but even that time, if work must be clocked, is work-bound.[9]

Godbey directs his critique at the very notion of modern leisure and at what he sees as the 'anti-leisure' character of much of it; for him 'anti-leisure' is

> activity which is undertaken compulsively, as a means to an end, from a perception of necessity, with considerable anxiety, with a

high degree of time-consciousness, with a minimum of personal autonomy and which avoids self-actualisation, authentication of finitude.[10]

What then are their positive understandings of leisure? For Godbey, clearly leisure has to do with the obverse of the various aspects he sees in anti-leisure, and we should note in this context that this implies a low degree of time-consciousness, among other things. He sees the concept of leisure as having a 'residual' sense, that is, 'surplus time after work, sleep and other necessary activities'; a 'prescriptive' sense, that is, 'a condition of the soul'; and a 'normative' sense, that is, 'as time free from work and other duties which may be used for relaxation, diversion, social enrichment or personal development'.[11] And he briefly illustrates his notion of the leisured life by referring to 'those who have traditionally had leisure in our society: the philosopher, the artist, the theologian, the musician',[12] in the course of suggesting that future leisure 'professionals' and recreation service providers would do well to study such models, rather than continue to reproduce the prevailing conceptions and practices of 'anti-leisure'.

De Grazia is a good deal more forthcoming and eloquent about his positive understanding of what leisure really is and ought to be, offering a classically-derived combination of what Godbey refers to in his 'prescriptive' and 'normative' concepts. Thus 'leisure is a state of being free of everyday necessity, and the activities of leisure are those one engages in for their own sake. As a fact or ideal it is rarely approached in the industrial world.[13] 'Neither busily active to some end nor supremely uncritical of whatever passes by, the activity of leisure chiefly refers to the activity of the mind.'[14]

I have a great deal of sympathy with these critiques of the natural attitude to leisure in modern industrial societies. However, I retain some distance from them on the subject that concerns me most in this paper which is that of the experience and concept of time and its relationship with leisure. Godbey clearly implies that a positive experience of leisure involves, among other things a low degree of time-consciousness. De Grazia develops the same kind of argument at much greater length. In his view the positive experience of leisure 'real' leisure in the appropriate normative/prescriptive senses, is antipathetic to time. Thus he writes:

Not being divided up by time, leisure does not suffer the fragmentation that free time does. Any stopping or shrinking of an activity in leisure is intrinsic, done for the doer's own interest.[15]

Time has its stop in leisure. In free time it becomes an obsession. . . .
For leisure the idea (of time) simply does not apply.[16]

De Grazia's and Godbey's critiques of the conventional understandings of leisure are well aimed and well taken, particularly those of the
domination of the leisure experience by a clocktime consciousness and
calculativeness which is nurtured in and necessary for employment,
and those of the work-dominated definition of leisure in terms of a
notion of free time and free-time zones. But in contrast to their
positive view of leisure as involving an antipathy to time, I wish to
suggest that leisure cannot be understood *without* reference to time.
Clocktime and calendar time, the socially objective forms of time, are
not the only, nor necessarily the most significant, forms of time in a
human life and experience. Rather, they need to be assessed in
comparison with 'inner', subjective or 'lived' time.

De Grazia and Godbey's critique is well aimed at the work-time and
clock-time consciousness that so often characterises so-called leisure
experiences in so-called 'free time'. But the weakness of their account
is that they imply, unnecessarily, an extension of this critique to cover
all time-consciousness. As against this I will, below, draw attention to
some features of time consciousness implied in leisurely activity in
principle and in retirement in particular.

II   LIVED TIME, WORK AND LEISURELINESS

In this section I shall look briefly at lived time in two senses of 'doing
time'. The first sense is foundational and is related to the very business
of what it is to exist in and through a 'lifeworld' as such.[17] The second
sense is critical, is derived from the discourse of imprisonment,[18] and is
evocative of much about the experience of our employment-
dominated world, the sense that in or out of work in this world one is
'doing time'. Overall I suggest that a fundamental notion of 'lived time'
is necessary to understanding 'work', whether in the broad sense of
activity as such or in the narrow sense of employment activity. This
notion involves three aspects which I shall call 'time-structure' ,
'time-stress' and 'leisureliness', and these are introduced in this
section. In the main body of the section the experiences of
employment and unemployment are discussed specifically in terms of
my analysis of lived time and in particular in so far as they involve
time-stresses of pace and fixation. Finally, I outline a concept of

'leisurelines'. In the following section of the paper the experience of retirement will be introduced to illustrate and to explore applications for this concept.

(a)   Lived Time as Fundamental

Whatever else people and human groups do, they order their activities and experiences temporally. In a basic and broad sense they structure, or 'do' time. This seems to me to be an ontological given about human beings[19] and about their collective life.[20] As such it is as important to understand on behalf of – and is a fundamental for – the human and social sciences as are other ontological givens about the human condition. For the human sciences it is undoubtedly important to understand that (and how) people, first, are embodied;[21] secondly, need to work to survive physically and mentally;[22] and thirdly, are communicative/language-using entities.[23] But it is at least equally important for those scientists to understand that (and how) people are 'in' time and how they 'do' time,[24] and how all psychological and sociological phenomena – taken in the very broadest senses to include all personal, interpersonal, historical, cultural, political, economic and other such phenomena – display temporality in their very existence as orderly forms of experience and action.

Lived time may be conceptualised as the cognitive and practical foundation on to which the clock-time and other societal time measurement systems are superimposed: which carries them and applies them.[25] Just as oral communication 'precedes' writing psycho-developmentally and phenomenologically, so lived time precedes societal time orders such as clock-time.

The temporal order both framing and emergent within lived experience may be thought of as a 'time-structure'. *Time-structure* at one level is a fairly simple and commonsensical concept, although at another level its implications are more complicated and will need to be unpacked more systematically. From the point of view of any person – conceived as a conscious, perceiving and active entity, operating in a meaningful environment (their 'lived world' or 'lifeworld')[26] – the *primary structure* of lived time displays a unity of the three commonsensical dimensions *present*, *past* and *future*. The dominant experience of *the present* is not that of any instant 'now', but that of a *flowing* and emergence of experience, activity, involving both emergence and routines, and of changes and continuities in the environment, during the course of particular short-term episodes[27] of mental and also (usually) bodily activity. The present, that is, the time in which I am 'currently' doing whatever I am doing, based on the short-term episode, may be measurable as a period within the day, or the day ('today') as a whole, or possibly as some somewhat more extensive period in which flow and emergence can be orientated to. The *past* and the *future* comprise medium- and long-term domains defined in part in terms of the present and its flow. Thus the past comprises, in part, the sources and history of present action, the endurance and continuity of the actors' identities, their autobiographies, the history of the action-environment and so on.

Similarly the future consists in actual and possible directions of the flow of current activities – the temporal 'place where' the actor is going in the medium and long term, the possible places where s/he might end up if lucky, or not too careful, the preferable, possible and probable future of the relevant action environments, and so on.[28] This time-structure, with its three dimensions of time-consciousness, can be called *primary*, in the sense that humankind is unintelligible without it. But we can also allow that there are and must be *secondary* structures. For any given individual these form part of his/her 'situation' and they map on to the primary structures. They have to do with the categories and measurements of time present in any given group, culture or civilisation.[29] For our purposes, and for purposes of life in modern societies, these secondary structures into which we are all socialised consist of skills and interests in both *'telling' the time*, by means of clock and calendar, and also in *'keeping time'*, that is, synchronising personal activities with the time-tables and time-measurements of major institutions and organisations, principally those of employment.[30]

With this schema in mind we can develop the health and value aspects of temporality in terms of an axis running from negatively perceived experiences of 'time-stress' or 'anti-leisure' to positively perceived experiences of 'leisureliness'. These concepts can be usefully applied and illustrated with reference to both employment and unemployment, and also to the sense of 'doing time' that they often involve.

(b) Time-stress, In and Out of Work

In terms of the earlier analysis, time-stress consists in distortions, deformations and in a certain sense a *loss* of structure, in the primary personal time-structure. Thus the present, the flow of the present, and access to futures and pasts, may be disrupted in various ways by the disruption, for whatever reason, of the temporal order embodied in such things as need-satisfaction routines; waiting/deferment abilities; effective act-sequencing; synchronisation; ability to account for action; understanding of 'appropriate' age and life stage-roles.

Time-stresses can often be caused by the repression of some or much of the personal time-structures including clock-time measurements and motivations. Time-stress from this or any other cause often shows up in two general sorts of perceived problem. First, there is the problem of *the pace* of the flow of activities and experience, whether perceived to be 'too fast' or 'too slow'. Secondly, there is the problem of a fragmentation of the structure available in the flow, a loss of structure. This can occur in the form of *fixations*. For instance there may be a fixation on one of the dimensions and thus a lack of access and flow in attention and consciousness between the dimensions of past, present and future. Or, alternatively, there may be a culturally and psychologically inappropriate fixation in an age-role/life-stage-role.

Some of the most severe kinds of mental health problems can display, and indeed largely consist of, these sorts of time-stress phenomena, generally of pace and fixation. Problems of pace, for example, passivity and hyper-activity, and of fixation, such as fixation on a problem in the past, or having no sense of future, have been attested to in various phenomenological studies (for example, compulsive neurosis, manic-depression, and long-term imprisonment).[31] We can now consider some time-related and particularly 'time-stress' – related aspects of experience in and out of employment, before proceeding to an outline of the more positive aspect of temporality, that of 'leisureliness'.

Pace-related time stress

It is a common experience – which we seek to monitor and control– to find ourselves occasionally doing or experiencing things at an uncomfortable pace – too fast or too slow for comfort. In some parts of our lives we may intend to create pace-related time-stresses, but this is under controlled conditions. So, for instance, the person who buys a new car may decide to check out its top speed and what it feels like to drive at that speed. Or the athlete may try to run at maximum speed when training, either to check her progress or as part of a programme of controlled overloading aimed at increasing her running ability.[32]

The pace time-stresses arising from employment and its absence are more imposed and less controllable than these examples.[33] They can present themselves to the individual as requiring activities and/or experiences which are persistently either too fast for comfort or too slow for comfort. It is a common observation that one of the various stresses and pressures of most jobs is the time-stress caused by the pressure to do things speedily and to meet 'deadlines', the uncomfortably hectic busy-ness of the 'rat-race'. Here the time-stress is the over fast pacing of activities and experiences. In contrast, one of the various stresses of being unemployed or retired, it is commonly claimed, is that of having nothing to do, of being bored and 'idle', having 'too much' time with too slow a pace and with a need to 'kill' or 'fill' the time. Here the time-stress consists in the over-slow pacing of activities and experiences. Personality types can make a contribution to the experience of discomfort and dissatisfaction with the pace of activities in these three situations. For instance, part of the initial crisis, the feeling and experiencing of 'loss' involved in enforced unemployment or retirement, results from the encounter between, on the one hand, a person who has been socialised and trained for a long period into a fast pace and the demands of life in employment and, on the other hand, the very different and usually much slower pace and demands of life outside employment.

Fixation-related time stress

At all stages in the life-cycle and in all age-roles it is important for mental health and well-being that, while sustaining access to the three dimensions of time-structure, the flow of activities and experience in the present be capable of being seen as directional and as 'going forwards'. This involves notions of 'progression' and 'having a future', rather than those of having no obvious direction which involve 'stagnating', 'going backwards', 'regression', 'having no (or an extremely uncertain) future', and so on. The two dimensions of present and future are tied together in ways that are possibly more important for understanding psychological/mental health than the undoubted importance of 'having a past' and of the past-present relationship.[34] So, while a sense of 'having a future', in terms of both imminent directions and longer prospects, is vitally important for mental health in youth and mid-life it is arguably no less important, in appropriately modified ways, in old age.

There are problems attendant, then, on 'living in the past', or 'living exclusively in the present' in ways in which access to directionality and emergent possibilities is cut off. Such fixations serve to fragment the time-structure and re-route the experience of flow in it in ultimately disturbing and debilitating ways. As far as past and future go, such disturbances may consist of exclusive attachments to those dimensions, either as such, or in so far as they contain idealised typifications of a self and its situation in preceding or succeeding age-roles and life-stages. We may have a fixation on memories of our childhood and wish to be a child again, or we may resent and avoid the fact of growing old and fixate on an inappropriate young or mid-life image of ourselves.

Employment and *unemployment* are tied together almost symbiotically in reality, in definition and in most people's conceptions of both of them, as 'job' and 'job-loss', rather in the way that notions of health and ill-health, and rationality and irrationality are similarly tied together in logic and opinion. The classical studies of blue-collar unemployment in the 1930s[35] support the negative view of unemployment. This view is still supported in studies of contemporary blue-collar unemployment.[36] But taking the big and controversial step of setting aside problems of income loss, for the sake of the argument, it is possible to regard blue-collar unemployment as not so much a 'loss' which people may have a fixation upon, but of a relief from job stresses, or even, more positively (in white collar studies), as a welcome opportunity either to find another and more satisfying job, or to engage in more satisfying unpaid work or leisure activities.[37]

Further relevant examples of the time-stress of fixation in the world of employment would be the relative absence of the future (for example, the lack of a 'career structure' for low-skilled blue-collar workers), together with their required attention to 'the present' in highly repetitive and programmed tasks. Relevant examples in the worlds of unemployment and retirement would be the shock and 'loss' experiences commonly associated with each of them. These involve a fixation on the past, an inability to relate in an animated way to the present and an unwillingness to consider the future other than as feared and uncertain. Such fixations are normally eventually overcome and a fully functioning experience of time-structure and flow is usually recovered. But it is worth noting that this recovery is also itself an experience of time, in that 'it takes time' and tends to unfold in a typical sequence of steps.[38]

Retirement is often conceived along lines similar to unemployment as a loss experience on which people can fixate.[39] Since it involves permanent and irremediable, rather than the possibly temporary and remediable, job-loss, the experience of loss and the fixation problem might be assumed, if anything, to be greater in retirement than in unemployment. However, there is room for a more positive view of retirees and their world.[40] The time-structures and time-stresses constructed around being 'in and out of work' are not necessarily merely replayed in retirement with a slower and more melancholy air.[41] Retirees learn how to cope with job-loss and free time more or less successfully, sooner or later. The 'wisdom' of old age may be disempowered and disregarded in modern times, but none the less it remains a resource for rethinking personal and communal values and attitudes to living. Part of such wisdom may be said to involve the time-consciousness attendant on the temporal ordering of experiences and activities in retirement. In turn, an important part of the characterisation of such time-consciousness may well be its capacity to avoid time-stresses and the anti-leisure of the 'in and out of work' world. From the negative resonances of considering the way in which we 'do time' in this latter world we next need to consider more positive conceptions of what a leisurely time-consciousness might be and how it might be displayed in the project – characteristic of retirement – of 'passing the time'. First, then, the notion of leisureliness.

(c) Leisureliness in Lived Time

If leisure is to be held to have any real basis in experience, it seems to me that that basis lies in a quality of the temporal ordering of experience, that of *leisureliness*.[42] This can be seen as a subjectively valued and reflectively monitored and enhanced form of lived time-consciousness. In principle, leisureliness is capable of accompanying any activity whatsoever, whether it is conventionally called 'employment', 'work' or 'leisure', 'free' or 'unfree', and so on. It is certainly *not* always and necessarily characteristic of activities called 'leisure' and conducted in 'free time'. In 'ideal type' terms, in a leisurely performance the actor orients mainly to the temporal aspects of the activity in question in three notable aspects, two concerning the present, and the pacing of the activity, and one concerning 'past' and 'future'.

First, 'in the present' the actor performs the action with a felt sense and attitude of *reserve and moderation*. That is, the actor is aware of the range and limits of possible durations and paces for the activity and performs it within limits, at less than the maximum pace and for more than the minimum duration. Secondly, also 'in the present', the actor acts with a felt sense and attitude of *patience and care*. That is to say, the actor is subjectively aware of 'giving time' or 'taking time', and on the side of the object of activity of giving 'the time *it* needs' to be done to a certain standard, or in a certain appropriate way. Finally, concerning 'past' and 'future' there is a felt sense and attitude of *reflective enjoyment*. That is, the actor takes time to enjoy or savour the activity in reflection, both in anticipation – in the course of preparing it – and in recollection – in the course of reviewing, remembering and reminiscing about it.

This schematic model can be used to analyse and evaluate the leisurely and non-leisurely forms of people's activities. We suppose that *leisurely activities* will reveal, in 'the present', aspects of reserve and moderation, patience and care, and in the 'past/future', reflective enjoyment in actions performed/anticipated. *Non-leisurely time-stressed activities* will reveal in 'the present' aspects of unreserved efforts or passivity, together with little sense of limits, impatience and carelessness; and either an unthinking hedonism or a calculating repression and over-control in the actions performed. As we have suggested above, time-stresses usually involve distortions of *pace*, and *fixation*, and in general tend to accompany repressions of primary structures by socially imposed temporal ordering and measurement such as often occurs in clock-watching and clock-timed employment situations.

Leisureliness can, in principle, be a feature of any substantive activity whatsoever, whether or not the activity is normally understood to be a 'leisure activity'. Any activity can in principle be performed in a 'leisurely' way. The experience of so doing is an experience of leisureliness. It may well be argued that there is an 'elective affinity' between activities which present themselves as having voluntary and intrinsically valuable characteristics and those that are most appropriate for undertaking in a leisurely way. But even actions that appear imposed, and even meaningless and valueless to the subject, such as some aspects of employment, can be oriented to in a way which selectively scans them for whatever opportunity they might provide, however minimal, for realising voluntary and intrinsic value aspects. In this way even highly routinised and alienating employment activities can occasionally be potential canditates for a leisurely performance.

So the view presented here is that there is a time dimension or continuum present at the heart of *all* activities, running from anti-leisureliness (time-stressed 'activism') to leisureliness. This makes it possible, and indeed necessary, to reconsider the definition of 'leisure' activities. I would be inclined to admit to the scope of that definition only those activities which are usually, or which can be reasonably readily, performed in a leisurely rather than in an 'activist' fashion. As noted earlier, conventional and commonsensical categorisations of such things as 'sport' as 'obviously' and automatically a 'leisure activity' on the one hand, and, on the other hand, various forms of employment as equally 'obviously' not a leisure activity need to be reviewed, and perhaps discarded, depending on their assessment in terms of the time-stress/leisureliness axis.

In terms of this axis it is possible to show that much modern sport – from that played by élite professionals down to that played by ordinary participants – all too often has an uncomfortably activist and stressfully hectic character to it, let alone the questions of whether it is enjoyable/unenjoyable, deadly serious/carefree, and so on.[43] The notion that sport can all too often become hard and dangerous 'work' rather than 'play' seems to me to find too little resonance in the 'philosophy of leisure' underlying much contemporary sport research and policy. This is particularly so regarding the implications and effects of 'unsporting' sport in educational, medical, psychological and sociological contexts. The promotion of sport as a form of *retirement* recreational activity[44] clearly carries health and welfare costs which need monitoring as much as any benefits it may also carry. Such 'activism' may carry costs for retirement lifestyles to the extent that they are successfully adapted to 'passing the time'.

III   LIVED TIME, LEISURE AND RETIREMENT

(a)   Retirement and Society

To begin with, it is worth noting some sociological factors which structure characteristic types of general retirement situations and hence impinge on and permeate the consciousness and experience of subjects charting their own personal ways through these situations. We can then 'bracket' these considerations and put them out of play to focus more directly and generally on leisure experience and the lived time dimensions in retirement.

Most retired people are also, in the conventional perception, 'old', although this seems set to change as the pattern of employment appropriate to post-industrial society emerges more clearly, a pattern that may well include significantly more 'early' and younger retirees than at present.[45] However, for the present it remains true that most retiring people are 'old', both in years and in social perceptions of age.

'Old age' may appear to be an exclusively biological phenomenon. In fact, it is also a sociological one, since the length and quality of old age is determined by the level and quality, the social organisation and distribution of medical, dietary, environmental and income resources.[46] In the advanced industrial and post industrial societies longevity is increasing, together with the length of time in old age that people can expect to be reasonably fit and healthy. For these societies the association of old age exclusively with physical decline, illness and death is becoming inappropriate to much of the actual experience of old and retired people.

While 'old age' is only a partially sociological phenomenon, 'retirement' is an exclusively sociological phenomenon and, as a mass experience, an exclusively modern industrial phenomenon at that. The timing of retirement, the nature of the break from employment, the quality of life in retirement are all in general determined by the development of the economy (the pattern and productivity of labour utilisation, the power of labour to command income and to save, and so on) and by the development of the state, particularly in its welfare functions (such as pensions and the levels of provision of housing and health care).[47]

But to say that retirement and old age are in important respects sociological phenomena should not be understood to imply a unitary or homogeneous form of experience for all old people and retirees. Nor does it imply that the elderly and retired statuses, whatever their actual growth, are positively valued by the rest of society. On the contrary, modern societies are evidently riven with social inequalities and prejudices along a number of axes, in particular (i) income and wealth; (ii) cultural skills, literacy, education, training and in modern cultural communicative competence; (iii) gender; (iv) ethnicity; and last but not least (v) age (or more accurately and long-windedly, perceivedly legitimate characteristics and implications of age-related *roles*).

So the retirement situation is characteristically different depending on one's position on these axes. Working- or middle-class women who have pursued a life working on home and family for a male partner who has been an employee cannot be said to 'retire' when the man does or in the same sense that he does. But obviously husband and wife share the experience in important senses. Their common domestic situation and lifestyle change, and, for almost all households containing retirees, people share in and have to adjust to a significant fall in their income and purchasing power, including purchasing power for leisure goods and services, for tourism, and so on. Finally, people have to get used to varieties of 'ageism': first, to intentional and institutionalised barriers and prejudices against the old; and/or, secondly, to a physical and social environment, urban and public spaces and services, which are rarely designed with their needs in mind; and/or, thirdly, in a minority of cases, to 'purpose-built' residential 'care' for the elderly which is often *careless* about people's individuality and which in some cases is positively damaging.[48]

(b) Time and Retirement

Having noted these sociological factors and without being complacent about them, we can now focus more directly and generally on the leisure experience and the time dimension in retirement, which are two important aspects of the 'lifeworld' for retirees.

So, in general, what do people typically do in retirement? This is not an easy question to answer as much of the research into this has been animated by, and to a significant extent hampered by, a prior and overriding concern to judge whether what people do is good for them. If nothing else, retirement is time 'free' from paid employment, it is the archetype in modern culture of a life lived in apparently totally 'free time'. And, indeed, the idea, at least for the retiring employee, that the retirement life – whatever else it promises – importantly promises, and indeed is *about*, a change in his or her time, is traditionally symbolically marked in the ritual gifts to the retiree of a gold watch. In this patronising symbol employers intimate to retirees that up until now the company has been the employee's time-keeper for its own purposes, indeed that it has bought, owned and disposed of the employee's time. But now the worker can be publicly acknowledged to have graduated to the new(!) responsibility of being his own time-keeper, and able to take control of his own time for his own purposes.

As time 'free' from employment, retirement is a period in which either one can, in a sense, become one's own employer and 'keep busy', or else can 'slow down' and have a rest as a reward for a lifetime of exertion. The risk of this latter option is that of declining into 'doing nothing', into passivity, and ultimately into total dependency, psychological as well as physical, upon others. The understandable concern to defend old people's autonomy and to guard against unwarranted dependency animates much research into retirement.

However, this concern tends to assume that evidence for autonomy is mainly to be found by perceivedly active behaviour. 'Passive' activity that does not appear to involve much active behaviour and activities that merely 'pass the time' tend to be much less recognised in terms of their possible contribution to autonomy and health. On the contrary, researchers often seem to assume that passivity and passing the time, to the extent to which they are even noticeable and describable, are problematic and indicative of incipient decline and dependency.

The thought carried forward into the retirement context from the previous themes in the discussion is as follows. Many retirement activities may well involve a real experience of leisure at their very heart to the extent that they regularly and substantially provide for a *leisurely* experience of whatever activities, however trivial or minimal, that are undertaken. In general and in principle, the tending and monitoring of long-cycle growth processes – such as in gardening, animal husbandry, child-care, teaching – can be held to require attitudes involving patience, the willingness to wait, and so on. So it is worth noting that gardening, caring for grandchildren and for pets are significant activities for the retired. Once again, in general and in principle, notions of craftsmanship and of the proper exercise of a professional competence are intimately tied, in ideals and norms, if not in actual practice, to the leisureliness concept and to its associated ideas of taking time and care and allowing the 'logic' of the task to dictate the pace and duration of activity. So it is worth noting that craftsmanlike hobbies and also a vocational sense of service to others, particularly family, friends and neighbours, are also significant attitudes and activities for the retired.[49]

What retired people *actually* do, in detail, day-to-day, to 'pass the time' – what their 'lifeworld' is – ironically, is barely visible in much research animated by what might be called the 'activistic' assumptions indicated above. What is really needed to answer the question about the activities of the retired (and also to give the philosophy or theory of leisure something to bite on or, less aggressively, hold a dialogue with) are descriptions of an ethnographic and phenomenological kind of these activities and of their ordering and recollection in experience. Some account is needed for the mundane and everyday lifeworld in the condition of retirement. What is likely to be found, I suggest, is that, at the very least the clock-watching, time-measurement and time-allocation of the dominant versions of mundane everyday life in pre-retirement employment (and leisure) is likely to be found to assume lesser importance in retirement. On the other hand, the lived time-structure in general and the temporality intrinsic in and specific to projects of activities is likely to assume a far greater importance in people's lives, together with a greater awareness of more gross and physically based time markers, such as days and seasons.

(c) 'Passing the Time': a Study

As an indication (and only an indication) of the kind of study that is needed here we can look briefly at Johnson's study[50] of long-retired men (based on interviews with two samples of working- and middle-class men in Sheffield). This study will also serve to illustrate some of the points of the discussion so far. Johnson found that the long-retired conceive of 'retirement' itself in terms of time, that is, as both being a finite period of time and as constituting 'one's own' time. Retirement as a time period was expressed as a period until death, or until ill-health becomes a problem. To most of the men this period was conceived to be about ten years (which matches well the statistics on the onset of health problems). It was viewed as a period of 'reward' and comparative freedom and autonomy in relation to their previous working lives. The perception that, in retirement, 'one's time is one's own' was found to inform retirees' attitudes, but it is notable that this was seen as time for work as much as for leisure. On the one hand, the men regarded retirement as a 'reward' and thus a well earned 'rest' from the rigours of employment. But on the other hand, this did not imply for them less 'work', rather a more relaxed and autonomous organisation of that work. Parkinson's Law that 'work expands to fill the time available' seems true for retired men.

Johnson's sample often expressed the rather surprising claim that they had never been so busy as in their retirement. One man commented, for instance: 'The days aren't long enough to do what I want to do, well like it's time to cut the roses back . . . the hedge wants trimming. I'm just waiting for the better weather to do these.' On the whole these samples did not provide evidence for a view of their lifestyles as either 'passive' or meaningless. Rather they were active in 'passing the time' in a self-organising and leisurely way. That 'passing the time' is a significant retirement project, is confirmed in Johnson's study and he found that it typically consists of investing meaning, time and effort, first, in what might be called the 'trivial pursuits' of the everyday round, and secondly, in long-standing leisure interests.

As far as the second form of 'passing the time' goes, that is, *'leisure' interests*, many chose to continue these into retirement, and thus to follow patterns already established earlier in the life course. However, this continuity did not involve an expansion of such activities to 'replace' work in employment. A minority may have significantly expanded their 'leisure' activities, including tourism, but also many reduced those leisure activities most closely associated with their 'lifestyle' while employed. This was either because these activities were to some extent work-related (golf, entertainments, 'working holidays') or were now too expensive to continue. The result of this is that most of the retired in the sample appeared to live lives somewhat distant from conventional formulations of a satisfactory lifestyle. But none the less their activities are largely meaningful and satisfying to them despite being capable of being glossed by most research as 'passivity' or as codeable in the 'remainder' box of time-budget surveys.

As far as the first form of 'passing the time' mentioned above goes – *'trivial pursuits'*, – small daily or intermittent tasks in and around the house or flat were found not only to 'fill in time', but to provide tasks that are meaningful, in that they are necessary and demand some rudimentary ordering of time. The main elements in the mundane and everyday lifeworld of the retired, which Johnson's study pointed up, were the temporal orderings associated with the activities of housework and meal preparation; walking and shopping; and gardening. A brief note on each is in order here.

Housework

Meal times in particular provided regular time 'signposts' in the day around which to order other activities. Meal times have a particular rigidity born out of long habit for the retired. Other tasks around the house were found to have more flexibility; for instance, cleaning may be done on a weekly basis with a routine easily changed to accommodate changed plans or spontaneous actions. Less regular tasks, such as decorating, were planned on a seasonal or yearly basis. Men previously involved in crafts were found to take a pride in completing such decoration or maintenance tasks to a high standard. Pride is taken in a 'job well done', one that has usually taken 'as long as it takes'. This unhurried approach means that apparently simple tasks can take considerable periods to complete. This is especially true in that they can often be left 'for a while' if they become irksome or if something else becomes attractive. For those who owned their homes this activity was often seen as either enhancing the next generation's inheritance or making the home a more comfortable place for all.

Walking

Far more popular (and somewhat ignored in the literature) are gardening and 'walking' as retirement activities. Johnson found that walking was often said to have a particular purpose, outside its own benefits, such as getting to a place for a 'view', or for fishing or, more instrumentally, for shopping. Shopping provided an excuse for casual social contact, and it was indulged to the full. 'Time-saving' supermarkets and so on were not favoured as these preclude the pleasant 'chat' or interesting sights that accompany frequent shopping trips. Shopping is, of course, a necessity for everybody, but for the retired it assumes a new meaning; it is still necessary, but it also becomes a 'pleasure'. Indeed, it shares some features with 'social centres' without the supervision and constraint of such organised social gatherings. Walking was recognised as 'necessary' for health, yet it also assumed a dimension of pleasant time consumption. A 'walk' can be as long as one likes, and only ended when weariness sets in or it is time for a meal. It has a 'logic' of its own.

Gardening

This was also found to exemplify many of the aspects of time consciousness we have been considering. For those who had a garden or an allotment it was a necessary activity; in a sense, it 'must' be done. Men used it as a way of getting out of the home and fulfilling an unambiguously masculine role (unlike shopping or housework, some aspects of which were resisted by men). It also had an imposed timetable of its own. The seasons demand particular attention be paid at particular periods. Thus the competent gardener (and indeed the decorator or do-it-yourself buff) must be aware of the passage of the seasons and make plans accordingly. These plans need not be precise to the week or day but sufficient to ensure that planting, pruning, propagation and so on are all completed at the correct season and in the best weather conditions. Considerable time can be spent in the garden and the summer months are the time for a great deal of activity tending the garden. This was not found to be obsessive activity, as it was punctuated by meals, visits, TV watching, rain and a host of other desired and undesired 'interruptions'. The tasks of gardening can be demanding, in the sense that they expand to 'fill' time when it is not being 'used' for other activities. In poor weather, especially the 'winter time' other tasks can be engaged in at the individual's pleasure.

Overall then, the home-centred tasks touched on make demands on the individual to plan time use within certain parameters. These parameters are set by the logic of the task and allow for considerable flexibility. Though the retired man may find he is 'very busy' that busy-ness contains little of the time-stresses found in employment. Rather the busy-ness is of the individual's making and is tailored to the desire of the individual.

These broad parameters – the period of retirement, the passage of seasons, weekly tasks and 'set' meal times – provide a backbone structure to the use of time in the lifeworld of retirement. Within this structure variations can be readily accommodated, things can be 'put off' if something interesting is on the television or friends call in a way impossible in employment. The attractions of this leisurely rhythm of life go a considerable way to enhance our understanding of the 'passivity' of the retired. Taking an active part in voluntary organisations, clubs and other 'activities', as advocated by various retirement experts (and gurus) could well be seen as unsatisfying (unpopular) options. This is because such activities require a commitment to a demanding and rigid timetable that the retired feel they have a right to avoid. The activities most favoured by those able to live the 'leisure lifestyle' are largely home-centred or require little commitment to a set temporal structure, and so tend to involve little commitment to others. Much more popular are activities that have a time structure of their own, that allow for spontaneity while also fitting into a planned future. Many tasks are 'leisurely' in that they demand a particular activity to be completed in a period that is limited by the logic of the activity itself (potatoes are best planted before November frosts, emulsion is best applied in dry weather). Also these tasks require establishing a structure for the future based upon the past and present conditions. The temporal structure goes beyond the day or week to much longer, although perhaps hazily defined, parameters that are always available for redefinition according to changing present conditions.

In conclusion, the retired are well able – given sufficient resources and security and assuming the social environment obstacles are not too imposing – to engage in a form of 'proactivity' and establish a 'rhythmic flow' to their period of retirement. This seems to be satisfactory in providing 'meaningful activity' without the felt necessity to 'replace' actively employment in their lives, except in so far as this represents access to income and its consequent possibilities for consumption. Indeed, the perception of a lack of time-stress is a factor to be taken into account in understanding the changing perceptions and status of the retirement role in our culture. Apart from the various prejudices against the old and the retired there may also be a growing envy for the attractiveness of well resourced retirement lifestyles, on the part of those currently in employment. Part of that attraction is not simply that the retired are rich in free time and hence leisure, but that they are also rich in knowing how to work in a leisurely way, how to use their time in a way which sustains and conserves, rather than drains and exhausts, their capacities to live and work. The attraction of retirement may be image or reality – and our brief look at some evidence suggests more the latter. But for those trapped in the work-dominated, clock-dominated and anti-leisurely modern worlds of employment or unemployment this attraction attests to their loss of disconnection from, indeed alienation from, their own lived temporality and in particular from their capacities to find time to take time or to pass time – their capacities for leisureliness in life.

CONCLUSION AND POSTSCRIPT

In line with the comments in the Introduction about the programmatic character of the paper it is unnecessary to do very much more here than merely lay the discussion down with a view to it being picked up at some other time and taken further. It is unnecessary to review what has been covered, as the Introduction has adequately previewed this. I merely add the following thoughts as a postscript.

The agenda for the 'philosophy of leisure' that my discussion points to obviously included questions about *the self-understanding of philosophy* as such, and also in respect of its role and place in the modern world. In this respect leisure may be more than just a phenomenon for description or a topic for debate. It may also – in the forms of 'leisurely activity' and 'the leisured society' and philosophy as a particular version of these, – be an opportunity to reflect on the sociological and praxiological conditions, resources and commitments required by the philosophical project, *however* that is constructed. This is because leisure must surely be a significant dimension of those conditions. Further, there is the thought that these conditions are in crisis, and hence need to be identified and, more than that, to be conserved and defended, renewed and developed.

The crisis issues from the combination of a number of historical tendencies loose in modernity. Among these are the drive towards an automated 'labour-saving' economy, the rise of life-threatening technologies and the accelerating pursuit of knowledge by sciences indifferent to value and over-specialised, which pose a threat to the human lifeworld and thus to the very conditions for the pursuit of the philosophical project. Some aspects of this crisis, particularly the relation between science and the lifeworld have received some attention in the phenomenological and critical theory traditions.[51] But the wider picture both of the combination of historical tendencies and their practical implications for those who would seek to defend the lifeworld, remains to be drawn. As part of this wider picture the place of leisure in the lifeworld, and the threats and opportunities history is posing to this place, need to be reflected upon and understood both for philosophy's sake and for the sake of the fate of our times.

The spirit of classical philosophy would counsel that such theory should be *for practice* and *for the 'good'* of the polis and of humanity. But it may be that an historically relevant practical reason about leisure or the lifeworld is beyond philosophy's grasp because of the peculiarities of philosophy's relationship with Time and History. Hegel observed that 'Philosophy in any case always comes on the scene too late to give . . . instruction as to what the world ought to be. The owl of Minerva spreads its wings only with the falling of the dusk.'[52] In his times this observation may have served to limit the hubris of enlightenment. But our times are threatened by nuclear and ecological 'dusks' that Hegel could never have anticipated. His sobering vision of Minerva's limits challenges contemporary philosophy and theory to prove him wrong, sets an agenda for its work and calls for its version of leisure to be reviewed. To me, Minerva's inability to rouse itself during *our* daylight, when there is evidently civilising work to be done, involves an indulgence in an 'academic' version of leisureliness and bad timing – a version which contemporary humanity can ill afford. Better late than never? Perhaps. But better still to be timely.[53]

Notes

1.   M. Roche, *Phenomenology, Language and the Social Sciences* (London, 1973).

2. For example, P. Friedlander, *Plato* (Princeton, N.J., 1969); S. de Grazia, *Of Time, Work and Leisure* (New York, 1962).
3. This latter issue is not taken further in this paper, but for a relevant discussion see M. Roche and B. Smart, 'Time, Leisureliness and Social Futures', in A. Tomlinson (ed.), *Leisure, Politics, Planning and People*, vol. 4 (London, 1986).
4. See de Grazia, *Of Time, Work and Leisure*.
5. H. Cunningham, *Leisure in the Industrial Revolution, 1780–1880* (London, 1980).
6. S. Parker, *Leisure and Work* (London, 1983).
7. M. Rose and S. Ward, 'Time Gentlemen, Please', *New Socialist*, May/June 1984, pp. 16–19.
8. Roche and Smart, 'Time, Leisureliness and Social Futures'.
9. de Grazia, *Of Time, Work and Leisure*, p. 326.
10. G. Godbey, 'Anti-leisure and Public Recreation Policy', in S. Parker *et al.* (eds), *Sport and Leisure in Contemporary Society* (London, 1975) p. 46.
11. Ibid., p. 46.
12. Ibid., p. 52.
13. de Grazia, *Of Time, Work and Leisure*, p. 327.
14. Ibid., p. 348.
15. Ibid., p. 348.
16. Ibid., p. 347.
17. A. Schutz and T. Luckmann, *The Structures of the Lifeworld* (London, 1974); Roche, *Phenomenology, Language and the Social Sciences*, and 'Social Theory and the Lifeworld', *British Journal of Sociology*, vol. 38, no. 2 (1987) pp. 283–6.
18. S. Cohen and L. Taylor, *Psychological Survival* (Harmondsworth, Middx, 1972).
19. H. Bergson, *Time and Free Will* (London, 1910); E. Husserl, *The Crisis of the European Sciences and Transcendental Phenomenology* (Evanston, Ill., 1970); M. Heidegger, *Being and Time* (London, 1967); P. Fraisse, *The Psychology of Time* (London, 1964).
20. G. Gurvitch, *The Spectrum of Social Time* (Dordrecht, 1964); A. Giddens, *The Constitution of Society* (Cambridge, 1984).
21. M. Merleau-Ponty, *The Phenomenology of Perception* (London, 1967); Giddens, *The Constitution of Society*.
22. K. Marx, *The German Ideology* (New York, 1969); M. Jahoda, *Employment and Unemployment* (Cambridge, Mass., 1982).
23. G. Mead, *Mind, Self and Society* (Chicago, 1967); P. Winch, *The Idea of a Social Science* (London, 1958); Roche, *Phenomenology, Language and the Social Sciences*; J. Habermas, *Communication and the Evolution of Society* (London, 1979), and *Theory of Communicative Action*, vol. 1 (London, 1984).
24. A. Schutz and T. Luckmann, *The Structures of the Lifeworld*; E. Jaques, *The Form of Time* (London, 1982).
25. Jaques, *The Form of Time*; M. Roche, 'Lived Time and Clock-work Culture' *Philosophy of Social Science*, vol. 17, no. 3 (September 1987) pp. 443–51.

26. Schutz and Luckmann, *The Structure of the Lifeworld*.
27. R. Harré, *Social Being: Theory for Social Psychology* (London, 1979); Jaques, *The Form of Time*.
28. E. Minkowski, *Lived Time* (Evanston, Ill., 1970); J. Roth, *Timetables* (New York, 1963); S. Lyman and M. Scott, *A Sociology of the Absurd* (New York, 1970).
29. Gurvitch, *The Spectrum of Social Time*; N. Luhmann, 'The Future Cannot Begin: Temporal Structures in Modern Society', *Social Research*, vol. 43 (1976) pp. 130–52.
30. E. P. Thompson, 'Time, Work, Discipline and Industrial Capitalism', *Past and Present*, vol. 38 (1967) pp. 56–97.
31. V. von Gebsatell, 'The World of the Compulsive', in R. May *et al.* (eds), *Existence: A New Dimension in Psychiatry and Psychology* (London, 1958) ch. 8; L. Binswanger *et al.* (eds), *Existential Analysis* (London, 1958) chs 7–9; Minowski, *Lived Time*; Cohen and Taylor, *Psychological Survival*.
32. A. Patmore, *Playing on Their Nerves: The Sport Experiment* (Port St Paul, 1979).
33. M. Roche, 'Time and Unemployment', forthcoming in *Human Studies*.
34. Minowski, *Lived Time*; Luhmann, 'The Future Cannot Begin'.
35. M. Jahoda *et al.*, *Marienthal: The Sociography of an Unemployed Community* (London, 1972); E. Bakke, *The Unemployed Man: A Social Study* (London, 1933).
36. Jahoda, *Employment and Unemployment*.
37. D. Fryer and R. Payne, 'Protractive Behaviour in Unemployment: Findings and Implications', *Leisure Studies*, vol. 3 (1984) pp. 273–95; S. Fineman, *White Collar Unemployment* (Chichester, 1984).
38. There is a variety of analytic descriptions in the literature on the subject; for example, J. Hayes and P. Nutman, *Understanding the Unemployed* (London, 1981); C. Parkes, *Bereavement: Studies of Grief in Adult Life* (Harmondsworth, Middx., 1975).
39. S. Parker, *Work and Retirement* (London, 1982); E. Cummings and W. Henry, *Growing Old: The Process of Disengagement* (New York, 1961).
40. N. Johnson, 'Passing the Time in Retirement', unpublished paper, delivered at the British Society for Gerontology Conference, 1984.
41. W. Grossin, 'The Relationship Between Worktime and Free Time and the Meaning of Retirement', *Leisure Studies*, vol. 5 (1986) pp. 91–101.
42. Roche and Smart, 'Time, Leisureliness and Social Futures'.
43. M. Roche and B. Smart, 'Governing Bodies: an Analysis of the Rationalisation of British Sport Policy and Administration', unpublished paper.
44. Sports Council, *Sport in the Community: The Next Ten Years* (London, 1982).
45. A. Walker, 'The Social Consequences of Increasing Early Retirement', *Political Quarterly* (January 1982) pp. 61–72.
46. E. Midwinter, *Redefining Old Age* (London, 1987).
47. C. Phillipson, *Capitalism and the Construction of Old Age* (London, 1982).
48. A. Norman, *Aspects of Ageism* (London, 1987).

49. M. Abrams, *Beyond Three Score and Ten* (London, 1980); Parker, *Work and Retirement*, and *Leisure and Work*; J. Long and E. Wimbush, *Continuity and Change: Leisure around Retirement* (London, 1985); M. Bernard, *Leisure in Later Life* (Stoke-on-Trent, 1985).

50. Johnson, 'Passing Time in Retirement'.

51. Husserl, *The Crisis of the European Sciences and Transcendental Phenomenology*; E. Paci, *The Future of the Sciences and the Meaning of Man* (Evanston, Ill., 1972); Habermas, *Communication and the Evolution of Society*, and *Theory of Communicative Action*.

52. G. Hegel, *Philosophy of Right* (Oxford, 1952) pp. 12–13.

53. I should like to thank my colleagues at Sheffield University, Nigel Johnson in particular, but also Barry Smart and Professor Alan Walker, for their suggestions and contributions over a period of time on ideas developed in this paper. Section III (c), pp. 71–4, above derives both from Nigel Johnson's 'Passing Time in Retirement' (1984) as indicated, and also from 'Passing the Time: Time, Leisure and Retirement' (1986), an unpublished paper which we jointly authored. In all other respects responsibility for the ideas contained in this chapter, and for their weaknesses, remains mine.

5

Personal Being and the Human Context of Leisure

ALEC GORDON

The aim of this paper is to carry out a philosophical intervention in the area of leisure theory. My concern in doing so is to argue the thesis that the proper philosophical context for theoretical reflection on the phenomenon of leisure is to pay due regard to the overall human context of the world of meaning which constitutes and is constituted by authentic personal and social-cultural creativity. The broader philosophically significant political context of the latter is that form of political constitution and organisation of civil society which enables the realisation of authentically meaningful leisure activities, that is the best modes of life which it is considered worthwhile to lead.

This paper can be considered as a philophical intervention in two ways. First, it carries out a metacritique of a particular social constructionist theory of leisure – that of Chris Rojek in his *Capitalism and Leisure Theory*.[1] Secondly, building on this critique, it puts forward a radical philosophical view on personal being and the human context of leisure considered as a constitutive human praxis.

CRITIQUE OF *CAPITALISM AND LEISURE THEORY*

The nub of my criticisms of Rojek's sociological approach to leisure can be briefly stated thus: In maintaining that the social reality of leisure resides in the fact that it is constructed out of relations which are relations of power, Rojek excludes from view the human agents who actually experience these power relations. In other words, his relational-constructionist perspective reduces the identity of the human agent who actually experiences leisure activities – which, Rojek asserts, are experiences of pleasure – to a dynamic configuration of external relations of power. Thus, the pertinent

80

context of leisure so conceived is one of extrinsic power relations. This reductionist approach towards the theoretical construction of the phenomenon of leisure is supported by adherence to a definite metatheoretical position. With the aim of emphasising the relational aspects of human history and interaction Rojek recognises the dual character of society and human praxis. The metatheoretical position Rojek calls upon to characterise the latter is that of Roy Bhaskar who, in his *The Possibility of Naturalism* writes: 'society is both the ever-present *condition* (material cause) and the continually reproduced *outcome* of human agency. And praxis is both work, that is conscious *production* and (normally unconscious) *reproduction* of the conditions of production, that is society'.[2] For his part, Rojek adds to these metatheoretical assumptions his own to the effect that the relations recognised by Bhaskar have to be considered *processually* – that is, as occurring in real historical time.

Despite adumbrating this metatheoretical base, nowhere in his book does Rojek deal with and *develop* a theoretical view of the human agent who, to stress, actually experiences leisure relations. This omission is perhaps not surprising since Rojek avowedly states that he is not interested in what he refers to as the *nominalist* tradition in contemporary sociological theory – namely phenomenological symbolic interactionist and ethnomethodological theories – that is, precisely those sociological approaches which are attempts to theorise human social action in its intrinsic dimensions as experienced by individuals conceived as social actors. Instead Rojek elects to concentrate in *Capitalism and Leisure Theory* on sociological theories in the *realist* tradition. By the 'realist tradition' Rojek means 'an approach to social study which regards society as irreducible to its constituent parts' (p. 8). Recognising that there are problems with the ways in which realist models have formulated the relationship between society and the individual, Rojek rejects outright the view that the individual is somehow 'outside' of society or that this selfsame socially abstracted individual is free to act according to his or her will or, again, that the individual is the ultimate locus of social reality. As well as rejecting any such idealist methodological individualism, Rojek also repudiates the one-sided deterministic view that individuals fulfil the omnipotent will of society in their thoughts, actions or feelings. Against these polarised conceptions of the relationship between the individual and society Rojek is at pains to emphasise the relational, interactional dual-aspect character of history and human praxis. Society conceived as both condition and outcome of human agency and praxis viewed as production and reproduction of social relations considered processually is, for Rojek, the metatheoretical conception of the social context of all human practice.

According to this account it may seem that Rojek has provided a comprehensive dialectical, material and historical approach to the study of all and any social action, including leisure practice. If this is, in fact, so, how then can it be objected that he has failed to deal adequately with the *human* context of individual action and personal being? The clue to the failure of Rojek's theoretical practice lies, I would argue, in the characterisation of his sociological approach to leisure as being an adequate 'objective' one. Let us consider, in his own words, Rojek's 'position on the essential considerations for an objectively adequate sociological approach to leisure' (p. 9) which he sets out in the last chapter of his book. In this last chapter, entitled 'The Sociology of Pleasure', Rojek divides his discussion of leisure as a phenomenon of pleasure into three sub-sections: 'Self and Selflessness', 'Leisure and Pleasure' and 'New Rules for the Sociology of Leisure'. He commences the chapter sceptically citing examples of the point of view that leisure rules are often associated with the experience of personal authenticity in the modern sociological literature on leisure. Rojek then comments: 'This view of leisure as something which the self possesses to exploit and develop represents a distinctively modern approach to the theory of leisure.' He is unable to accept such a viewpoint because he rejects the view that leisure is a phenomenon which has either a social or a personal essence. On the contrary, for Rojek, leisure is neither a social nor a personal entity as such; it is a set of social relations and structures – or practices, actions, behaviour, forms, rules.

Under the sub-heading of 'Self and Selflessness' Rojek offers the opinion that 'The conjunction of the concept of self-realisation with leisure is an adult view' (p. 174). Whereas adults have leisure, children merely play. Socialisation is the replacing of the unstable transitoriness but inventiveness of childhood with the renunciatory and sublimatory self of the adult state. Leisure forms in modern societies have, then to be understood as residing in the structural opposition between the adult world and the world of children.

Rojek next considers the opposition between the adult self and the selflessness of childhood with respect to the historical emergence and the organisation of leisure forms in advanced societies. He focuses attention on the medieval phenomenon of the carnival as representative of the mass experience of selflessness which is now lost to us today.

With, however, the rise of the mercantile-industrial bourgeoisies in European society and the private, egoistic ideology of possessive individualism, selflessness as a mass carnivalesque form declined and gave way to modern collective kinds of ultimately privatised leisure forms.

In the next sub-section of the final chapter, entitled 'Leisure and Pleasure', Rojek restates one of the main recurring themes of his book – that leisure relations should not be studied as relations of self-determination and freedom but, on the contrary, as relations of permissible behaviour. For Rojek 'What is considered legitimate and illegitimate in them is the socially produced effect of structural rules of pleasure and unpleasure' (p. 177). Here again, then despite his reference to the 'self' and leisure Rojek proposes a cause-effect description of leisure relations. It doesn't matter that, drawing upon Weber and Freud, the economy of pleasure in modern, rationally administered societies has positive 'effects'. What is at issue is that the social context of leisure is conceptualised in quasi-positivist terms as a social context of 'rules' which are understood as the resources for both regulation and innovation in leisure activity. So, yet again, Rojek's theoretical position is constructionist and relationist in reductionist terms notwithstanding his metatheoretical (ostensively dialectical) approach to comprehending society and praxis. Rojek seems to be unaware that there is a contradiction between his metatheoretical assumptions and his practice of substantive theorising. In other words, in his attempt to construct an objective sociological account of leisure he fails to realise in his actual theoretical practice the neo-Marxian theoretical assumptions which he adheres to. Rojek's theorising is corrigible, then, because he fails to theorise the subjective (personal) side of leisure relations – that is, society as the continually reproduced outcome of human *agency*. Consequently Rojek's practice of theorising amounts to one of reduction and not one of dialectical mediation between the metatheoretical assumptions which he adopts and his practice of substantive theorising.

What conception of the relations between the levels of metatheory and theory can help us to appreciate this contradiction in Rojek's theoretical practice? István Mészáros had recently written on the relations between metatheory and theory as follows:

> The level of 'meta-theory' cannot be separated *in principle* from the theory itself; it is only as a *moment* of analysis that it can be separated, but it must then be reintegrated again in the *overall*

synthesis. That is to say: meta-theory is an integral dimension of all theory, and not a privileged department governed by radically different principles. There can be no coherent theory without its own, specific meta-theoretical dimension and *vice-versa,* there can be no meta-theory . . . which is not deeply rooted in a set of theoretical propositions inseparably linked to determinate social *values.*[3]

According to this succinct account of the relations between metatheory and theory the criticism can be levelled against Rojek that he fails in his theoretical practice to carry out the *overall synthesis* of the reintegration of his metatheoretical assumptions and his substantive theoretical construction of the phenomenon of leisure considered as a privileged sociological object of study. Consequently he offers a severely impoverished account of the social context of leisure praxis which should, I would argue, be properly theoretically conceived as a human context – that is, one that foregrounds a place for constitutive processes in leisure praxis. Rojek's exclusion from a theoretical view of the subjective side of leisure relations in their creative moment of human praxis means that he has deliberately omitted to consider one of the (to call upon his own way of putting it) 'essential considerations for an adequate objective sociological approach to leisure'. The strategic exclusion of leisure as a creative moment in the formation of personal being – which has determinate social conditions of existence – is manifest in Rojek's forthright assertion that 'Leisure experience is not an essence in human societies but an effect of systems of legitimation' (p. 178). Here in a nutshell is Rojek's acceptance of an objectivist social constructionist characterisation of the phenomenon of leisure in capitalist society which rejects any naturalistic or empiricist view that constitutive human agency is a crucial moment of leisure praxis.

Rojek's adherence to a social constructionist-relationist theory of leisure is encapsulated in his proposals for 'New Rules for the Sociology of Leisure' with which he ends his book.[4] Here he dissociates himself from the two main sociological attempts to explain the phenomenon of leisure which he heuristically divides into two polar types.

On the one hand, there is the resolute bid to reduce composite relations of leisure to a finite sum of essences or particles. On the other hand, there is a bold attempt to penetrate beyond the apparent shapelessness of people's experience to hidden structures which explain the surface relations of everyday life . . . each attempt is associated with fundamental errors in theory and research. The attempt to reduce leisure relations to their constituent parts produces the 'leisure with society' syndrome. Equally, the attempt to impose logically consistent structures upon leisure practice seems to end in reification; everything that happens in society is explained as a consequence of the deep structures of social life.' (p. 179).

Rojek's relational-constructionist approach to leisure means that in rejecting these twin reductions he commits himself to another contradiction-reduction which is this: his refusal to consider one of the constituent parts of the ensemble of leisure relations – that of praxis – as a *constitutive* moment in this ensemble means that he reifies his structural-dynamic conception of leisure. This theoretical reduction-ism is ironical, considering that in his 'New Rules for the Sociology of Leisure' Rojek includes a place for what he conceives of as innovatory leisure action. In each of his four rules he cedes the initiative to the possibility of socially transformative leisure practice. In his first rule, for example – *'Leisure activity is an adult phenomenon which is defined in opposition to the play world of children'* (p. 180) – he admits into his description the qualification that leisure relations can break down or be transgressed. Who actually contests the social controls and constraints over potentially transgressive leisure praxis Rojek does not say. According to his constructionist-relationist theory, the possiblity of contingent transformations of leisure relations *qua* regulative rules can only be conceived as an 'effect' of the breakdown of the systems of legitimation of which leisure experience is an 'effect'.

In his second rule, which states that *'Leisure practice is an accomplishment of skilled and knowledgeable actors'* (pp. 180–1), the limits to the possibility of socially and personally authentic leisure praxis are set by the competence of the adult self viewed as a skilled knowledgeable actor who can manipulate social rules understood as resources for innovation as well as forming the basis for critical departures in leisure practice. The context of constrained-regulated or innovatory leisure practice is here conceived as a configuration of social rules, the novel transformation of which is considered an act of social 'manipulation'. Manipulation, then, is behaviour which counters social conditioning. The creative moment of human leisure praxis is here reduced to a contrived theoretical behaviourism which is seriously proposed as a radical conception of the objective context of leisure practice.

In his third 'new rule' for the sociology of leisure – '*The structure and development of leisure relations is an effect of legitimation rules of pleasure and unpleasure*' (p. 181) – Rojek finally reiterates his thesis that 'Leisure relations are not relations of freedom. On the contrary, they are relations of power whose dynamics and subjective meaning reflect the historically structured economy of pleasure in society' (p. 181). In the extended interpretation of this third 'new rule' Rojek states that pleasure and the self are aspects of the social structure, changes in the distribution and intensity of which can be examined historically. Here once again the identity of the self is contextualised with respect to relations of social structure which Rojek postulates as its external, necessary conditions of existence. Thus it is not the relatively, let alone the radically, autonomous self which experiences leisure but the self considered only as an 'aspect' of social structures. Human agency, then, is reduced to externally determining social structures. It is social structures, conceived as 'effects' of systems of legitimation understood as relations of power, which 'act' and not the individual self.

Finally, in the fourth 'new rule' – '*Leisure relations must be sociologically examined as dynamic, relatively open-ended processes*' (p. 181) – Rojek argues that privatisation, individuation, commercialisation and pacification, as the four trend-setting tendencies in the organisation and dynamics of leisure, have, in combination, operated to 'project the self, the individual body, to the forefront of leisure action and experience' (p. 181). In tune with his metatheoretical assumptions – that society is both the condition and the reproduced outcome of human agency, and praxis considered processually, is both conscious production and unconscious reproduction – Rojek proposes that these organising trends are historically contingent processes which provide the basis for new initiatives and counter-developments. But what constitutive, counter-determining role does conscious leisure praxis have in instigating and maintaining the latter? Rojek does not say; in fact, he is unable to answer this question because his practice of substantive theorising only allows him to conceive of individual agency or collective action as aspects of social structure. In this theoretical context of dealing with the dynamic, relatively open-ended processes of leisure relations he, in fact, refers to individual structures. Here, then, agency again is ascribed to social structures; it is not an intrinsically actual or even potential attribute of individual creative human agency – as Rojek's metatheoretical assumptions imply.

DEVELOPMENT OF THE CRITIQUE

In the preceding section of the essay I have taken issue with Rojek because he offers what I consider to be a reductionist theoretical explanation of leisure arguing that it is an 'effect' of systems of legitimation which in essence are power relations. I have also pointed out the contradiction between his metatheoretical assumptions and his practice of substantive theorising. The crux of this contradiction is that, despite ceding a place for human praxis in his metatheory, this place is either assimilated or reduced to the *structural* conditions of actual or possible constitutive agency. In other words, Rojek's theory emphasises 'structuration'[5] at the expense of an adequate theory of human action. His metatheoretical stress on human *agency* and praxis as work is not realised in a *constitutive* theory at the substantive level. The result is a theoretical behaviourist conception of leisure which one-sidedly deals with its social construction at the expense of a constitutive view of human leisure praxis understood as a social process which provides the conditions for the formation of personal and collective being.

This, in condensed form, is my criticism of Rojek's theoretical sociology of leisure which he argues for in his *Capitalism and Leisure Theory*. I want now to develop this critique further on three related fronts. First, I intend further to take issue with Rojek's constructionist-relational view of the human agent. I propose to do this drawing upon Richard Wollheim's criticisms of constructionist-relational theories of the human person which he puts forward in the first chapter of his *The Thread of Life*.[6] Secondly, I shall place a question mark against Rojek's conception of 'individuation' which, it will be recalled, along with privatisation, commercialisation and pacification, is one of the four trend-maintaining tendencies in the organisation and dynamics of leisure practice. I shall bring Rojek's conception of individuation in question via consideration of Rom Harré's theory of modes of individuality which he develops in his *Personal Being*.[7] Thirdly, I shall question Rojek's conception of socialisation calling upon John O'Malley's formulation of this key sociological concept which he propounds in his *Sociology of Meaning*.[8]

First, then, to intensify the criticism of Rojek's conception of the construction of the self. What I have been arguing is that, despite Rojek's allotting a place for human praxis *qua* productive work in his metatheoretical assumptions, his actual practice of substantive theorising has no place for praxis considered as a constitutive moment of human agency. Specifically, leisure behaviour is theoretically constructed by Rojek as, to reiterate, an 'effect' of systems of legitimation (permissible and impermissible behaviour) which are tantamount to relations of power. That is, the identity of human praxis is reduced to a set of external relations which 'structures' this identity. The reductionist theoretical effect of this view of social causation is that active human agency is conceptually represented in behaviouristic terms in a problematic of the 'production' (structuring) of 'effects'. Richard Wollheim lucidly points out the fallacy in such a theoretical move. In chapter 1 of *The Thread of Life* entitled 'Living', he raises the following objection to a constructionist-relationist account of the person.

> By a constructionist theory I mean a theory . . . that holds that everything that needs to be said about the events that make up the life of a person . . . can be said without introducing the person who has them. On a constructionist theory a person arrives on the scene only when there is a set of suitably interrelated events, then the person is or is identical with that set. The person appears *deus ex machina*, and the *machina* is the unity-relations. On such a theory to say of a single event that it is an event in some person's life is just to say that it is a member of an appropriately interrelated set of events of the kind that make up a life.
>
> By contrast, a non-constructionist theory is a theory that maintains that no event in a person's life, even taken singly, can be adequately described without introducing the person who has it. There is always some person who integrally enters into any event that is of the kind that makes up the life of a person.   (p. 16).

Interpreting Wollheim's characterisation of the opposition between constructionist and non-constructionist theories of a person's life with reference to Rojek's sociological account of leisure, it can be said that the event of an individual's experiencing some activity as a leisure activity is contextualised with respect to, or rather is reduced to, what Rojek considers the pertinent set of relations that make up an individual's life – that is, the appropriate configuration of power relations which are the determining and controlling conditions for leisure relations theoretically conceptualised as systems of legitimation – of permissible and impermissible behaviour. Thus any theory that confines itself to the relations between the events that make up a life is, according to Wollheim, one that is incomplete because it does not make reference to the person who experiences the event-relations. For Rojek leisure experience does not constitute an identity-relation in itself. Leisure practices are not assigned any constitutive moment independent of the construction-relations which structure them. The identity conditions for leisure experience are conceptually represented in Rojek's theory as a unity-relation of power relations conceived as systems of legitimation. But, argues Wollheim, identity is not relation – is not and could not be a unity-relation precisely because the terms between which identity-relations are required to hold are not the parts of a person's life. It is the person who provides the terms to the identity-relation.

Wollheim's endeavour in *The Thread of Life* is to ask and philosophically respond to the question 'What is it to lead the life of a person?' The asking of this question leads Wollheim to ask the related question 'What is a person's life?' It is in this fundamental interrogative context that Wollheim puts forward the criticism of constructionist-relational theories of the person that they take the symptoms of a specified set of unity-relations for an essence. In Wollheim's words: 'That which a person's life derives from the way in which it comes about they treat as itself constitutive' (p. 21). But construction in this sense which Wollheim criticises is not constitution. Far from it – indeed, constitution by definition cannot happen to a set of unity-relations extrinsic to a person whose identity as a person is reduced to them by a constructionist theory. In the case of Rojek's theoretical practice this means that constitution cannot be attributed to the systems of legitimation, to the power relations of which leisure behaviour is a structured 'effect'. Nor can constitution be assigned to the social structures of privatisation, individuation, commercialisation and pacification of which the self which 'experiences' leisure activity is only an aspect.

In addition to having adopted Wollheim's critique of constructionist-relational theories of the person for my own critical purposes in this essay I now want to draw upon a sophisticated social constructionist account of the personal self to further call into question Rojek's on human identity with particular reference to his conception of 'individuation'. The account I am referring to is, as I have already indicated, Rom Harré's theory of modes of individuality in his *Personal Being*. Rojek introduces the term 'individuation' in chapter 1 of his book which is entitled 'The Structural Characteristics of Modern Leisure of Practice', when he is discussing the sub-theme of 'The Organisation of Leisure in Modern Capitalism'. As already mentioned, Rojek itemises individuation as one of the four deep-rooted historical tendencies which give contemporary leisure relations their organisational form. The other three tendencies Rojek recognises, it will be recalled, are those of privatisation, commercialisation and pacification. Rojek defines individuation as referring to 'the historical and material processes which demarcate the individual as a specific person who is publicly recognised as separate and distinct from others' (pp. 19–20). For Rojek the foundation of the individuated personality is laid in the socialisation process and leisure relations contribute further to this differentiating process. In fact, says Rojek, 'The specialisation and differentiation of persons finds a corresponding reference point in the specialisation and differentiation of leisure pursuits' (p. 20). However, by making individuals different and separate, individuation makes people more subject to control and the leisure industry encourages and reinforces the narcissism of the individuated identity. From a Marxist standpoint, says Rojek, the consumption of commodities has the effect of further separating and differentiating individuals. This process of alienation masks shared life conditions and marginalises how these conditions are produced and reproduced.

Now, as far as it goes this account of individuation is acceptable, but, critically considered, it fails to give an adequate theoretical conceptualisation of the actual processes which demarcate the individual as a specific, publicly recognisable person. To be sure, Rojek's privileged area of concern is to intervene critically in the field of sociological accounts of leisure, but, even given that this is his elected area of study, he fails to deal with the constitutive distinctive personal aspects of the total individuation process. As an example of a developed theory of the specialisation and differentiation of persons, I want to discuss briefly the important contribution to this topic made by Rom Harré in his book *Personal Being*. For Harré *consciousness, agency* and *autobiography* are the three unities which make up our personal being. Together personal being as *formal* unity (consciousness), personal being as *practical* unity (agency), and personal being as *empirical* unity (autobiography) are able to account for the formation of individual identity which, for Harré, is realised in two complementary powers which we have as human beings: the power to display ourselves as socially unique and the power to create novel linguistic forms making individual thought and feeling possible.

The implications of Harré's theory for a developed view of individuation is that it does not take the individual as a given formal or substantive unity, but theoretically distinguishes the different unities which are the product of the conditions for the personal constitution of an integrated self. Thus regarding the analysis of leisure the differentiation of personal being into the above mentioned three unities would need to be accounted for by a detailed differential analysis of leisure activities which, so to speak, correspond – necessarily or contingently – with these three unities of personal being. However, rather than there being any simple empirical correlation of leisure pursuits and the assumed but never theoretically specified differentiation of persons, there needs instead to be a dialectical understanding of how, in sociological actuality, modes of personal being are constitutive of *themselves* via the participation of the individual in different leisure activities. As well as providing the theory for an individual psychology commensurate with this task, Harré also provides in *Personal Being* a view of the human-social context of the modes of formation of personal being as one comprised of a limiting and/or an enabling *moral* order. Such an approach to the human context of action as being essentially a personal and moral one can indeed be presented as a serious alternative to Rojek's constructionist-relational account of leisure behaviour theoretically conceptualised as an effect of systems of legitimation which are relations of power. A social theory of leisure which was informed by Harré's sophisticated Kantian-derived theory for an individual psychology[9] would theoretically represent the phenomenon of leisure as involving the *possibility* that the voluntary engagement in leisure activities *could* be concerned with the personal-moral development of the individual as part of a moral order in a determinate social context. Such a social theory would, of course, have to take into account the sociological fact that in contemporary late capitalist society, leisure is certainly, in part, a phenomenon of social control.[10] As Henry Lefebvre analyses in, as he calls it, 'the bureaucratic society of controlled consumption', there are two distinct types of leisure which are structurally opposed: first, leisure integrated with everyday life and conducive to profound discontent, and secondly, the prospect of departure, the demand for evasion, the will to escape through worldliness, holidays, LSD, debauchery or madness.[11] Such a soberingly realistic view of leisure in contemporary late capitalist society makes one think that, despite apparent mystifying illusions to the contrary, the systematic sublimations which are called leisure amount to nothing but a compensatory domain of distractions which cater for hedonistic pleasure-seeking.[12] From this debunking standpoint leisure conceived as authentic individual or social cultural creativity seems to be an embarrassingly presumptuous idealistic point of view to hold to. However, as a counter-viewpoint to the view that leisure is essentially only a compensatory realm of sublimatory and hedonistic pleasure-seeking, the critical idea of Agnes Heller to the effect that the perennial task of all philosophy is *to constitute a world*[13] can be brought to bear because it highlights the necessity for a radical philosophy to pose the 'possibility' of an 'ought' against currently what there 'is'. Thus, in the domain of leisure it could be argued that the repressed potentiality for authentic leisure praxis resides in the always pregnant possibility that, far from only being a compensatory realm of pleasure-seeking distraction and sublimation – which in many instances is what leisure undoubtedly is – the engagement in multifarious leisure activities can be recognised as both a means and an end to the formation of individual or social being which can intrinsically involve creative cultural action as well as the satisfaction of physical being.

Already in this essay I have referred to Rojek's conceptualisation of 'socialisation'. The context of this reference was his discussion on the formation of the adult self out of the apparently selfless self of childhood. To reiterate, Rojek argues that, as far as leisure behaviour is concerned, the process of socialisation in modern society is, in effect, the replacing of the selflessness of childhood with the renunciatory and sublimatory self of the adult state. Although Rojek espouses Marxian derived metatheoretical assumptions very early in his book, it is the influence of Michel Foucault's conception of power which eventually leaves its mark on his practice of substantive theorising towards the end when he constructs his 'Sociology of Pleasure' (chapter 8) and, in particular, when he puts forward his 'New Rules for the Sociology of Leisure' (pp. 178–81). Despite the criticism of Foucault's work which Rojek spotlights in the brief critical assessment (p. 157) which appears at the end of the short section devoted to a consideration of 'Foucault and Leisure' (p. 150ff.) – that is, that his conception of power is protean and therefore imprecise and, given his 'proposition that history is the effect of the "play" of power' (p. 157), that there are serious conceptual problems regarding the status of the human subject – he is still prepared to appropriate Foucault's ideas about the government of the body for his own critical project. Thus, departing from his Marxian metatheoretical assumptions, Rojek ends up equating the socialisation process with regimes of the government of the body.

Another influence on Rojek which can be discerned is that lying behind, or rather superimposed upon, the four trend-maintaining tendencies in the dynamics of leisure practice, namely privatisation, individuation, commercialisation and pacification, are Foucault's four regulatory principles of the social administration and control; in short, discipline, over whole populations as well as individual bodies – individuation (of private space), coding (prescriptions on social conduct), routinisation (the subjection to programmed schedules) and synchronisation (or activities according to strict divisions of labour and networks of commands). Thus, in advanced urban-industrial societies the socialisation process has, in Rojek's words, 'projected the self, the individual body, to the forefront of leisure activities and experience' (p. 181). It is the political economy of the body, then, as part of the historically structured economy of pleasure, in capitalist society, which finally occupies Rojek's theoretical attention.

The influence of Foucault's ideas on Rojek's practice of substantive theorising has the reductionist consequence that the 'body' is metonymically substituted for the individual self. Corresponding to this substitution is the identification of 'leisure relations' with 'relations of power' and, in turn, with another metonymic substitution – that of 'legitimating the rules of pleasure and unpleasure' for 'relations of power'. The socialisation of the adult self which experiences leisure/pleasure is thus characterised in a concatenation of displacements, identifications, metonymic substitutions and reductions which are all manifestations of the theoretical principle that 'the self is an aspect of social structures'. Ultimately, then, it has to be re-emphasised that, despite the stress on society being the outcome of human agency in his metatheoretical assumptions, Rojek's actual practice of theorising excludes the very possibility of leisure being conceived as a mode of cultural praxis. Just as the term 'meaning' does not figure in Rojek's theoretical sociology of leisure, neither does he use or develop any concept of culture. In chapter 5 of *Capitalism and Leisure Theory*, which is devoted to 'Neo-Marxist Approaches to Leisure', Rojek does mention the notion of culture when he briefly considers the work of the University of Birmingham Centre for Contemporary Cultural Studies on leisure, but here it loses out in prominence to the associated terms in contemporary neo-Marxist discourse of 'hegemony' and 'consciousness' (cf. pp. 132–4). This indifference to, or even tacit rejection of, the key theoretical notions of 'meaning' and 'culture' are symptomatic of Rojek's blanket repudiation of cultural idealism and essentialism in sociological theory in general. This indifference is also manifest in his view that the distinction between society and the individual is invalid. And yet Rojek's own practice of theorising contradicts this general denial. It does so by substituting the body/society distinction for that of the individual/society one. Whereas in Rojek's theoretical sociology the individual self is reduced to the body, albeit the socially disciplined body *à la* Foucault, society is equated with social structures, relations and process and the relations between them are predominantly conceptualised in terms of 'behaviour', 'practice' and 'activity'. All in all, then, in Rojek's theoretical sociology of leisure the function of the socialisation process is to construct the adult self which, as an aspect of social structures, as a special kind of prepared body, is projected on to the pleasure-seeking stage of leisure action and experience.

I shall now extend this critique of Rojek's conception of socialisation by way of focusing on the absence of any reflexive critique of this notion in *Capitalism and Leisure Theory*. I will do this taking a look at John O'Malley's *Sociology of Meaning*. The importance of O'Malley's consideration of the topic of socialisation for the critique being developed in this essay is that he grasps it as the focal problematic of a radical social theory which is attendant to its own practice of theorising. In fact, O'Malley conceives a consideration of the theme of socialisation to be the metaproblematic of a critically reflexive sociology in so far as it is not only concerned with the process of the social constitution of meaning but, at the same time, with its own process of meaningful theory construction inasmuch as it is itself a constitutive praxis. The radical imperative of the on-going appreciation that such critical reflexivity is endlessly necessary means that there is a need to ask what the lived implications are of any particular sociological practice in determinate circumstances. Just as, then, as Harré says, 'every . . . general psychological theory . . . must be assessed, not for verisimilitude, but in relation to some moral order, that is with respect to the kinds of lives belief in it enables people to live' (p. 284), so, too, must every social theory be considered with reference to the kinds of lives acceptance of and or belief in it enables people to live. Thus, faced with Rojek's theoretical sociology of leisure we have to ask how it relates to concretely experienced moral orders?[14] The answer to this question seems to be that in so far as Rojek's sociology of leisure is actually a social theory of pleasure in contemporary capitalist society – or, more specifically, of permissible and impermissible relations and experiences of pleasure – the internal (that is, critical and reflexive) assessment of the theory with respect to any given moral order does not actually arise. Radical normative considerations of the moral kind involved here do not apparently have any critical place in Rojek's theory – or rather, they do very much arise albeit in a highly mediated form. For example, an implied conception of a moral order which accords with Harré's concept is represented in the quasi-legalistic conception of permissible and impermissible forms of pleasure as well as in the acceptance or wilful manipulation of the social rules which govern leisure behaviour. Further, in so far as Rojek assigns a place for transformative, contestatory or transgressive action in the formulation of his 'New Rules for the Sociology of Leisure' he surely implies that deviation from, or even the subversion of, the social norms which govern leisure practice are the legitimate outcome of leisure socialisation. It is as if, to call upon Rojek's ideas, freedom in the domain of leisure is equated with getting involved in dangerous situations the result of which is to provoke the breakdown of incorporated adult leisure relations. To be sure, Rojek's own words imply that negative determination of the social controls and disciplines which are part of officially administered leisure relations is tantamount to the exercise of freedom in this sphere of individual and collective social life.

Paradoxically, then, what is pleasurable in Rojek's theoretical sociology of leisure is not conformity to the prevalent social rules which govern leisure practice but the active participation in breaking them down, altering them or going beyond them to produce 'new rules' of leisure in actual practice. The perverseness of this position apparently resides in Rojek adumbrating that the proper end of leisure socialisation is the pseudo-dialectical turnabout of the willed engagement in transgressive, contestatory or transformative counter-socialisation in the field of leisure.

The question has to be asked once again: What moral order is compatible with Rojek's theoretical sociology of leisure? That is, to enquire again, what kinds of lives does belief in his theory enable people to live? More specifically, it can be asked what kind of involvement in leisure activities is implied by Rojek's 'new rules'? Given Rojek's equating of leisure with relations of power, which are also systems of legitimation, the answer has to be a life which is conscious of this sociological construction of leisure. But what are the consequences of this knowledge for engagement in leisure practice? Surely either to conform pragmatically to the dominant social rules which govern leisure practice when it is so convenient or to act to delegitimate these rules. But is such duplicitous behaviour compatible with 'pleasure'? The asking of this question returns us to the standpoint of O'Malley which, to repeat, stresses that a radical sociology which is self-critical will be aware of the implications and the direct, if not also indirect, consequences of its practice for the processes of socialisation – which here have to include conscientisation, intellectualisation and even politicisation.

A further interrogation of Rojek's practice is in order at this point: does knowledge of a sociological practice and its products enable a life to be led which is one of the constitution of meaningful meaning, that is a worthwhile life which is informed by creative values, with respect to some life-enhancing moral order? In responding to this general question in Rojek's specific case I would submit that his theoretical sociology of leisure does not provide the intellectual means for such a cultural praxis of constitution because, above all, it does not have a conception of human agency which is informed by a non-reductionist theory of personal being. The absence of any critical reflexive conception of socialisation as an integral part of Rojek's sociology of leisure is the sign that it is not constructed to take account of the requirement that it be assessed in relation to not only the moral order which it, itself, contains and projects but also in relation to other moral orders which are entirely incompatible with it. This said, it has to be noted that it is surely an awareness of the normative implications of a practice of sociological theorising which is the condition for the sociologist to engage in a principled process of self-criticism which is also a process of self-understanding and self-constitution. The critical question any social theorist is obliged to ask, then, is this: What moral order do I wish to engender by my practice of theorising? That is, what kinds of lives would I wish people to lead if they were persuaded by, accepted and believed in my theory?

A theoretical sociology of leisure which is constructed with reference to a critical understanding of enabling, constraining or implied moral orders will be able to argue, on a principled philosophical basis, that, as radical cultural action, as the reassertion of creative, human self-constitution, leisure is, in O'Malley's words, 'the positive deviancy of personality' (ibid.). Leisure, then, as the projection of personal-cultural style into the field of leisure conceived as a field of enabling and constraining sociality, departs from and goes beyond any preconstituted and strictly regulative pattern of leisure socialisation. For O'Malley,

This means that however effectively a 'normative order' be

formulated, however persuasively propagated and coercively enforced, freedom finds play in the inevitably personal transignification of such patterning in its adoption and, consequently, in the equally personally styled transformation of the situation that is directed by it. At the radically theoretic level of morality, this is manifest through the theoretic style of what has traditionally been called wisdom and the practical style of what must be called fidelity.   (Ibid.)

RADICAL PHILOSOPHY AND LEISURE THEORY

Given the critique developed in this essay, a philosophical intervention in the area of leisure theory has to acknowledge the imperative of proposing what the possible 'ought' is as a repressed potentiality of what there currently 'is' which emphasises that the theoretical constitution of an authentic world of leisure, considered as a world of potential meaning constitution, must be assessed in the contexts of the moral, ideological, institutional, political and economic determinants on leisure activity. However, a radical philosophical view of leisure must not reduce it to one or other of the latter contexts but should always foreground an understanding of authentic leisure praxis as sensuous human practice and, simultaneously, as subjective meaningful activity experienced in an authentic institutional form of cultural *communitas*. Authentic leisure praxis, then, has anterior given conditions of social construction on which objective basis – and possibly against which – genuine leisure practice is constituted.

In her book *A Radical Philosophy*, Agnes Heller offers a neo-Kantian interpretation of radical needs which is relevant to a radical philosophical view of leisure and its human context. She writes that

The *ideal of the good* contains two aspects: the recognition of all needs and the satisfaction of all needs. 'Every need must be recognised' is a *constitutive idea*; 'Every need must be satisfied' is a *regulative idea*. We act under the guidance of regulative ideas and we accept the idea as universally valid; it is however part of the essence of regulative ideas that their observance is only conceivable as an *infinite process*.   (p. 168)[15]

Thus the need to develop one's personal or social being in relation to the material and cultural wealth of a society is a constitutive idea of the utopian human context of leisure, whereas the actual realisation informed by the belief that these specific leisure needs are authentic is a regulative idea. More recently Heller has written: 'The process of developing endowments into talents constitutes the "construction of the self". Every person is a self-made person for every person is a self-making person.'[16] In this philosophical context the terms 'constitution' and 'construction' reinforce each other, focusing on the process of self-development. It is this constitutive philosophical idea which provides the human context of the development of personal being – not forgetting in asserting such that the process of the developments of endowments into talents takes place in determinate limiting and enabling social circumstances. Thus leisure, considered in an Aristotelean sense as freedom form work, as the pursuit of good activities with which work interferes, is only positively constitutive of personal being in political conditions which enable the appropriation of the cultural means necessary for individual self-development.

Such a philosophical view of leisure as a constitutive human praxis is completely incompatible with and can only be opposed to the reductionist sociological view that leisure is a system of power relations conceived as relations of the regulative legitimation of permissible and impermissible behaviour. A conception of leisure praxis viewed as the development in concrete identity projects of the three unities of personal being – those of consciousness, agency and autobiography – on a mediated socio-biological foundation of physical being in determinate conditions of social being, is incommensurable with leisure behaviour conceived at the 'effect' or 'aspect' of social structures. The latter reductionist viewpoint ideologically coheres with the jaundiced sociological view that leisure is a phenomenon of social control in the late capitalist society of bureaucratically controlled consumption in which we live. To be sure, as has been discussed above, in this society leisure is either a compensatory form of integration into a fragmentary everyday life (including a vexing life of unemployment) or it is a compensatory evasion from the alienations of modern life. But the existing realities of these two structurally opposed forms of leisure do not exhaust the repressed potentiality of what authentic leisure praxis ought to be. It is the task of radical philosophy to mediate between the incorporated forms of hedonistic leisure behaviour and the authentic forms of pleasurable, enjoyable and worthwhile forms of leisure praxis which can be developed. In Aristotelean terms this means recognising that amusements or pastimes (*paidiai*), that is activities whose *raison d'être* is enjoyment, although having intrinsic value, are not equatable with *eudaimonia* (happiness), the most worthwhile life which should be led. *Scholē*, freedom from work, the positive pursuit of good activities, is equatable for the most part in our society with *paidiai* and the seeking after hedonistic happiness.[17] The domination of affective-emotive surplus needs and drives means that happiness, the highest good, conceived as the life of contemplation, is assigned to the realm of rational-cognitive action. Hence in our society there is a contradiction between the rational-cognitive as equated with the realm of work – in Aristotle's terms *àscholia*, the absence of leisure – and the rational-cognitive *qua* contemplation as the highest good. In so far as the latter is the repressed poteniality of the former, it is the task of radical philosophy to highlight this very repression at the same time as arguing the thesis that *eudaimonia*, as the ideal of the good, is the basic constitutive idea – even if this is not realised in practice as a lived regulative one.

What are the consequences of this diagnostic interpretation for the place leisure occupies in the development of personal being? In responding to this question it should be noted that Harré's three unities of personal being – those of consciousness, agency and autobiography – in their optimal (ideal) development is a constitutive idea, whereas their actual realisation in specific identity projects is a regulative one. The lived context of the latter is everyday life which, in late capitalist society, is both heterogeneous and based on the disjunctive unity between work and so-called freedom from work. In turn, and to state again, there is a structural opposition between leisure as compensatory evasion of or escape from it. Thus the cultural content of the forms of the unities of personal being have to be understood as being defined by the contradiction between work and leisure and the structural opposition between the two forms of leisure identified. Using Harré's terms it can be observed, in this connexion, that the formal unity of consciousness is subservient to the practical unity of agency, especially, and the empirical unity of autobiography, as these unities relate to an acquired socio-biological substratum of surplus needs and drives. In other words – and again calling upon Harré's concept – the power to create novel linguistic forms in order to express individual thought and feeling is subordinate to the power to display oneself as socially unique. Leisure, then, as freedom from work is equal in our society to the permissible forms of enjoyment and amusement but, above all, to the pursuit of pleasure and hedonistic happiness. The pertinent unity of formal consciousness which needs to be taken into account here is the cognitive legitimation of these forms of leisure behaviour and, in particular, what conceptions of self have been culturally internalised which appertain to the notion of 'freedom from work'. In remarking such, it is important to stress that just as everyday life is heterogeneous[18] so, too, are modes of leisure behaviour as part of the diversity of identity projects. However, it must not be forgotten that the real socio-cultural context of this heterogeneity is the structural opposition between the two forms of leisure as either integration into or evasion from everyday life. The reflexive task of a radical philosophical intervention in the domain of the construction of a theoretical sociology of leisure, then, is forever to draw attention to the fact that, at the same time as analysing this structural opposition, any such theoretical sociological practice is also part of the heterogeneity of everyday life and that its content has more or less constraining (even repressive) or enabling (freedom-engendering) consequences for the development of a human context for authentic leisure praxis.[19]

Notes

1. Chris Rojek, *Capitalism and Leisure Theory* (London, 1983).
2. Roy Bhaskar, *The Possibility of Naturalism* (Brighton, 1979) p. 8.
3. István Mészáros, *Philosophy, Ideology and Social Science: Essays in Negation and Affirmation* (Brighton, 1986) p. 14.
4. Cf. Anthony Giddens, *New Rules of Sociological Method* (London, 1976).
5. In a footnote – the last in Rojek's book – he says that his conception of 'structuration theory' has been influenced by the following works: Pierre Bourdieu, *Outline of a Theory of Practice* (Cambridge, 1977); Bhaskar, *The Possibility of Naturalism*; and Giddens, *New Rules of Sociological Method*; see also the bibliography to Rojek's book for further references.
6. Richard Wollheim, *The Thread of Life* (Cambridge, 1984).
7. Rom Harré, *Personal Being: A Theory for Individual Psychology* (London, 1983). This is the second in a trilogy of works which Harré has been writing on various 'ways of being'. The first volume was *Social Being: A Theory for Social Psychology* (London, 1979). *Personal Being* is the sequel to the latter and the third volume *Physical Being*, will be forthcoming from Basil Blackwell.
   More recently Harré has contributed to the development of social constructionist thinking regarding the study of the human emotions; see Rom Harré (ed.), *The Social Construction of Emotions* (London, 1986).

In particular, see his introductory essay, 'An Outline of the Social Constructionist Viewpoint' (pp. 2–14). See also in this volume Claire Armon-Jones, 'The Thesis of Constructionism' (pp. 32–56). Armon-Jones indiscriminately uses 'constitution' as a non-controversial synonym for 'construction' in this essay. In the present critical context I aim to distinguish between these two terms. In fact, I argue that it is necessary to do so for the reason that 'construction' is associated in the social constructionist paradigm with a deterministic conception of human agency. Alternatively the conception of 'constitution' which I propose takes account of relatively autonomous phenomenological-symbolic processes of agency with their own sufficient, if not necessary, conditions of existence. A dialect between interdependent processes of 'construction' and 'constitution', rather than an unreflective identity between them, is, I argue, what is necessary in order to develop a comprehensive and adequate social theory of personal and social being.

Social constructionism, although apparently a relatively recent paradigm in the field of social pyschology, has had a longer pedigree in academic sociology. Taking their theoretical precedents from Marx, Weber and Durkheim, Peter L. Berger and Thomas Luckmann, in *The Social Construction of Reality: A Treatise in the Sociology of Knowledge* (Harmondsworth, Middx, 1966), wrote what is probably the key contemporary study in this area. In this work Berger and Luckmann pose the following question as being central to sociological theory: 'How is it possible that subjective meanings *become* objective facticities? Or . . . How is it possible that human activity (*Handeln*) should produce a world of things (*choses*)?' The answer to this question, according to Berger and Luckmann, requires an adequate understanding of how the reality '*sui generis*' of society is constructed. If *The Social Construction of Reality* was a contribution to the sociology of knowledge, then Michael A. Arbib and Mary B. Hesse's *The Construction of Reality* (Cambridge, 1986) aims to develop an integrated perspective on human knowledge using theory and research in cognitive science, the philosophy of science, the human and cultural sciences, philosophy, theology, biblical and literary criticism and artificial intelligence theory. In addressing fundamental questions concerning human action in the world, and whether the space-time world exhausts all there is of reality, Arbib and Hesse endeavour to produce a coherent and integrated view of the individual and social dimensions of knowledge. The relevance of *The Construction of Reality* to my critical project in this essay resides in the fact that the authors 'seek to reconcile a theory of the individual's construction of reality through a network of schema or mental representation with an account of the social construction of language, science, ideology and religion' (p. ix). Thus Arbib and Hesse's thinking on the appropriation, transformation, translation and production of schemata is relevant to the cognitive aspects of the construction and development of the three unities of personal being identified by Harré – namely (to anticipate my discussion of them in the main text of this essay), those of consciousness (formal unity), agency (practical unity) and autobiography (empirical unity). To further anticipate my critique of Rojek's *Capitalism and Leisure Theory* in the main text and, in particular his decision not to deal with phenomenological, symbolic, interactionist and ethnomethodological sociological approaches to leisure – what, ambiguously, Rojek refers to as the 'nominalist' tradition – a work which deals with 'constructionist' and 'realist' models of making sense is B. C. Thomason's *Making Sense of Reification: Alfred Schutz and Constructionist Theory* (London, 1982). This work is also important because it contains a sustained critique of Berger and Luckmann's *The Social Construction of Reality* with respect to their emphasis on the active side of social construction at the expense of the passive, apparently reifying aspects of social action. Thomason argues for a positive view of the latter in the context of the general sociological understanding that needs to take account of the ways in which we both make sense *with* each other and, at the same time, of one another.

8. John B. O'Malley, *Sociology of Meaning* (London, 1971); and Agnes Heller, *A Radical Philosophy*, trans. James Wickham (London, 1984), and *Beyond Justice* (London, 1987).

9. Harré's theoretical project in *Personal Being* is post-Kantian in that he acknowledges that 'Kant's philosophical innovations can be looked on as contributions to a general psychology in which the unities of experience are accounted for through the application of the doctrine of synthesis' (p. 15). On the basis of the precedent of Kant, Harré says: 'My project is Kantian in that I do not believe that the unities that are the basis of selfhood are given in experience. However, unlike Kant, I believe that it is possible to give an account of their origin in empirical terms, but the terms are social. Contrary to Kant, who held that transcendental objects had only transcendental properties, I hold that at least some transcendental objects have social properties' (p. 27).

10. Cf. Alan Tomlinson (ed.), *Leisure and Social Control*, a workshop of the British Sociological Association/Leisure Studies Association Joint Study Group on Leisure and Recreation, organised and hosted by the Centre for Contemporary Cultural Studies, University of Birmingham (London, 1981).

11. Henri Lefebvre, *Everyday Life in the Modern World*, trans. Sacha Rabinovitch (Harmondsworth, Middx, 1971) p. 85.

12. Cf. Colin Campbell, *The Romantic Ethic and the Spirit of Modern Consumerism* (London, 1987), especially chapter 4: 'Traditional and Modern Hedonism'. In contradistinction to the delegitimating view that leisure is merely hedonistic pleasure-seeking, Campbell tacitly argues that leisure is hedonistic consumerism, the understanding of which should be focused on the strain between dream and reality, pleasure and utility. The critical background to this interpretation turns on an understanding that, in Campbell's view, the cultural logic of modernity is not to be equated with the vicissitudes of rationality, of calculation and scientific experimentation, but resides in the structure and expressions of passion, of creative dreaming and longing.

13. Heller, *A Radical Philosophy*, p. 1.

14. Cf. Harré, *Social Being*, in which he argues that all students of the human sciences must accept the general moral obligation to offer an explicit account of the political consequences of their work.

15. The distinction between 'constitutive' and 'regulative' is, of course, taken from Immanuel Kant's *Critique of Pure Reason*, trans. Norman Kemp Smith (London, 1933) A509/B537 and A568–9/B596–7.

16. Agnes Heller, *Beyond Justice* (London, 1987) p. 309.

17. Cf. *The Ethics of Aristotle*, trans. J. A. K. Thomson (Harmondsworth, Middx, 1953), and *The Politics*, trans. T. A. Sinclair, revised and re-presented by Trevor J. Saunders (Harmondsworth, Middx, 1981). For a recent discussion of Aristotle's conception of leisure (*scholē*) in the wider philosophical context of an examination of the concepts of hedonistic happiness and *eudaimonia* and the relationship between them, see Elizabeth Telfer, *Happiness* (London, 1980). Needless to say, the contemporary relevance of Aristotle's philosophy is disputable. See, in this regard, Ellen Meiksins Wood and Neal Wood, *Class Ideology and Ancient Political Theory: Socrates, Plato and Aristotle in Social Context* (London, 1978) chapter V: 'Aristotle: Tactician of Conservatism'; Amelie Oksenberg Rorty (ed.), *Essays on Aristotle's Ethics* (Berkeley, Cal., 1980); Joseph Owens, 'Is Philosophy in Aristotle an Ideology?', in Anthony Parel (ed.), *Ideology, Philosophy and Politics* (Waterloo, Ontario, 1983) pp. 163–78; and Stephen R. L. Clark, *Aristotle's Man: Speculations upon Aristotelian Anthropology* (Oxford, 1985) p. v.

18. Agnes Heller, *Everyday Life*, trans. G. L. Campbell (London, 1984) chapter 4, pp. 47ff.

19. I would like to thank Pamela Anderson of Mansfield College, Oxford, for her help in the preparation of this essay.

6

Another Way of Being: Leisure and the Possibility of Privacy

MARTIN DAVIES

The world is everything comprised by the horizon of our understanding and our freedom. For as it is ordinarily experienced, it is at once a continuous stream of images formed by our mind and a kaleidoscope of desires and obligations, expectations and commitments, shaped by our intentions and refined and checked through social interaction. But the world is also the historical situation in which we inexplicably find ourselves, set down as we are in the latter part of this late dark age, the daunting twentieth century. Our enigmatic insertion into history we experience as being someone's child or someone's parent; as being younger than some, older than most; as having seen less than some or being more worldly-wise than others; as being now less, now more advanced in the practice of institutions on which our existence depends. Often we feel that the historical world, unfathomable to us in its dreariness and confusion, draws in upon us like a long, dark midnight, but without the assurance of a following day; and that the store of possibilities it holds against the future must be running low as it draws mankind inexorably towards the ultimate moment of self-knowledge in an ultimate self-encounter.[1] Inevitably, therefore, we feel that some of the colour is draining from the ever-shifting patterns we experience and suspect that some of its scope and variety are no longer obtainable. Now it is against this background that the concept of leisure has to be defined, and as a response to some disconcerting questions. For, in view of the aleatory predicament of human aspirations, what is the value of leisure for existence? There can be no doubt that we do have our leisure, as a moment's reflection on our own experience confirms. But how does leisure fit into this historical world? Indeed, in a world such as this, what is the point of leisure?

One answer may found in a poem written by Rainer Maria Rilke

(1875–1926) in the summer of 1908, entitled 'Der Leser' ['The Reader'] and published in the second part of his *Neue Gedichte* later the same year;

Wer kennt ihn, diesen, welcher sein Gesicht
wegsenkte aus dem Sein zu einem zweiten,
das nur das schnelle Wenden voller Seiten
manchmal gewaltsam unterbricht?

Selbst seine Mutter wäre nicht gewiß,
ob *er* es ist, der da mit seinem Schatten
Getränktes liest, Und wir, die Stunden hatten,
was wissen wir, wieviel ihm hinschwand, bis

er mühsam aufsah; alles auf sich hebend,
was unten in dem Buche sich verhielt,
mit Augen, welche statt zu nehmen, gebend
anstießen an die fertig-volle Welt;
wie stille Kinder, die allein gespielt,
auf einmal das Vorhandene erfahren;
doch seine Züge, die geordnet waren,
blieben für immer umgestellt.[2]

English prose version:
Who knows him, this man, who turned his face / away and out being to another / which only the rapid turning of full pages / sometimes rudely interrupts?
Even his mother would not be certain, / that it is truly he who reads there / something bathed in his shadow. And we who have our time in hours / what can we know of how much fell away from him, until / /
he looked up wearily: drawing up on to himself / everything contained in the book below / with eyes which, instead of taking / met with their yield the finished, ready-made world: like quiet children who, engrossed in play / learn suddenly of their surroundings; / but his features which were settled / remained forever changed.

Reading is, by any definition, a leisure activity: the poem confirms this. But Rilke's poem also tries to define what sort of an experience reading is; it tries to say what happens to someone who is at leisure. The poem shows that leisure is materially dependent on its opposite principle, the world of work, while the sphere of necessities, utilities and purposes, represented here by the very book he holds, the artefacts we suppose to be in his room, the materially given world itself, ['die fertig-volle Welt, 1.12] are all shared by both spheres. It suggests, too, that leisure is not necessarily easy: reading, like any activity of our leisure, makes demands on our skills and interests, it requires concentration, lays claim to our attention even though, at the same time, it draws on a certain attitude of relaxation. But, above all, it confirms that leisure needs its own specific location in time and space: shown here (we infer) by a reading-lamp which casts the shadow, an armchair for the reader to sit in, a quiet room which others, the mother and the observer, going about their ordinary business, only pass through or pass by. In other words, the poem argues that leisure is another, divergent form of being.

This divergent character of leisure, its capacity to bestow on us a new unrecognisable identity [cf.11.1,5] is the key to defining what sort of an experience it is. Some would no doubt disagree. There have been many studies detailing the various ways in which socio-economic factors influence individual choices and opportunities for leisure activities. Few of them, I suspect, match the sweeping pessimism of Theodor Adorno's late essay, 'Freizeit' ['Free time'] (1969), in which he construes leisure as a source of consumption which benefits the entertainments industry and denies people the imagination necessary to make constructive use of what free time an industrial society does allow its work-force. His reason is that in an age of unparalleled social conformism it is difficult to see how people can be different from their social function.[3]

Even so, divergent forms of being occur – and reading is a case in point (even if Adorno says he takes reading too seriously to call it a hobby). Reading, like chess or, indeed, tennis or mountaineering, requires a specific location, requires its own time. This question of location, where reading is concerned, has particularly preoccupied George Steiner; it is worth quoting him because of his emphasis as much on the fact of divergence as on the physical hindrances and moral objections to it.

The economics, the physical environment of daily existence, particularly in the most technologically-advanced communites in the West, does not make for the personal acquisition of libraries in the old manner. The pace of being, the surrounding noise-levels, the competitive stimulus of alternative media of information and entertainment . . . militate against the compacted privacy, the investments of silence, required by serious reading. Self-bestowal on text . . . is a posture simultaneously sacrificial and stringently selfish. It feeds on a stillness, on a sanctuary of egotistical space, which exclude even those closest to one. Today's ideals of familial co-existence, of generational amity, of neighbourliness are parti-cipatory, collective, non dismissive.[4]

That experience consists of both work and leisure–however unequally determined by socio-economic necessities–establishes the fact of a divergent mode of being. That it is an existentially valid alternative is confirmed by the requirement of a special location, since this indicates not merely an empirically contingent divergence but rather points to the formal, *a priori* possibility of another mode of experience. In his essential analysis of the foundation of individual experience in modern times Kant construes space and time as the synthetic *a priori* conditions of understanding and experience. As long as we are conscious, we are conscious constantly of time and space and our perceptions are formed by these preconditions.[5] But it is also possible to argue – and our own self-reflection makes it necessary to add–that our consciousness of time and space is variable: the time we spend casually waiting for a train is structured differently from the time when we are late and struggling to keep an appointment – as might be revealed in our differing reactions to the same distraction, (say, someone asking us for directions) during these periods. To the extent that we are differently aware of time and space when we are attending to the social and economic demands of our life from when we are not, the divergence provides the formal possibility for an alternative way of being. Hence, leisure is not just a different kind of experience within a constant, transcendental time-space structure, but the converse: a modification of these preconditions of experience makes leisure possible, even necessary.

Consequently, without belittling the hindrances to the personal use of free time they describe, both Adorno and Steiner may be said to be victims of their own 'stringent selfishness' and impute too much passivity to their 'egotistical space'. Furthermore, it needs to be stressed that leisure may cast its spell over the world of work. In Rilke's poem the reader's mother and the observer are momentarily arrested in their daily business by the presence of the reader: in the former he gives rise to doubt, in the latter to admiration. In other words, leisure has the power to turn those at work, those still appropriated by their daily function, into spectators, into an audience. Leisure, even when it is exclusively self-engrossing, also elicits aesthetic attitudes from its non-participants. Certainly it seems that leisure is not a restrictive or a reductive concept; rather it mirrors existence itself. My contention is that if we wish to know what our existence is like and where we actually live, we should turn to leisure which, in coming to us in a time and space of our own, gives us another perspective on being.

How, then, is leisure experienced in relation to time? Leisure is, above all, the name given to the experience of our own time. 'Do this at your leisure' is synonymous with 'do it when you have the opportunity', that is to say: when you have time, in your own time. Except that it is a sobering reflection that hardly anyone has his or her 'own time'. On sundials and antique clocks the inscription *tempus fugit* reminds us that the days of our life are numbered. But the modern experience of time can no longer be adequately expressed by the topos of transiency, that exquisite, Horatian sentiment of evanescence which for so long pervaded European culture. When we speak of the modern experience of time, we refer to our experience of fragmented, yet often overlapping time-dimensions, caught up as we often are in 'the synchronous character of asynchronous events' ['die Gleichzeitigkeit des Ungleichzeitigen']. Who can be said to live in the same moment as anyone else, except in an external way in that we all appear in the same place at the same time? Our moral and intellectual values each have their varying genealogies, their heterogeneous correlates in our own life-history. These time dimensions, labyrinthine in their intersections in the mind of one individual, let alone within a society, are the fault-lines along which our world, the internal coherence of our experiences and projects, threatens to collapse, often does collapse, no matter how much we try through repeated rationalisations to shore it up.[6]

Certainly, the historical time in which we live is not our own. Perhaps only world-historical individuals (to use Hegel's intimidating phrase) can fashion an era to their own desires. But even then, powerful political figures are often little more than puppets of geopolitical interests which far transcend them. Ordinary individuals can only be significant in history through mass movements. But, paradoxically, as totalitarianism shows, the recourse by them to treachery and crime in the attempt to 'force the destinies of those excluded from official history into the memory of posterity' only leaves the individual more vulnerable and expendable.[7] But it is not just an intellectual deduction, it is also a truth of our own experience that each person is alone in history. How can any purely human aspiration survive against the mounting burden of the past whose shadow looms large across the future?[8] To be human is to be able to make projects; that requires some temporal scope, some material security, a sense of the future, and a degree of expectation.[9] But the time for our projects and the wider historical time in which political schemes are executed rarely concur: what expectation might a Jewish child have entertained in Nazi Germany? What progressive ideas are eradicated piecemeal daily in South Africa, Iran or Chile? (As if there were even any need to look so far afield for political decisions which eradicate the premises of humane culture.) For each person isolated in history, politics is fate. Politics is no more nor less than the effects of the ideas and intentions of a few people on millions of people. But across the world these millions react to the changes, suffering and upheavals these individuals cause as they would react to the effects on their environment of the vagaries of nature, such as storms, hurricanes and epidemics.[10] For this reason, resignation and retreat, an almost complete renunciation of the will, would be an understandable response on the part of an individual to the political inclemencies of the historical time in which he or she lives.

In our ordinary experience this historical time is experienced as a time to which we can see no end: it is a straight line, inexorable, unyielding. It is the time on which our existence as socio-economic entities depends. It is a capitalistic time, the time in which interest accrues, mortgages are paid off, leases expire, insurance policies mature. It is a time which regards the future as a long-term investment which requires the sacrifice of what we are now, the present as a raw material to be exhaustively exploited, the cultural and material resources of the past as a share-profit to be realised.[11] Moreover, this is the time of our social expendability and economic redundancy, as the institutions in which we are employed, along with the social needs they both serve and create, evolve in accordance with a time and world of forces which far transcend the temporal limits of an individual's life. Contemporary society makes it bad enough to grow old and disqualified from taking better advantage of its material achievements unheard of in one's younger days. But it also adds insult to injury when, because of this progress, it makes its victims feel useless and unwanted because it no longer requires them to participate in it.[12]

But, beyond those of history and society, there are other dimensions of time over which we have as little control. There is an intimation of cosmic time in the sublime prospect of the heavens at night or of mountain ranges, as much as in the grotesque nightmare of nuclear disaster: beyond history there is nothing like the time-scale of the physical processes of the universe for rendering human existence insignificant. And yet this cosmic time has an unexpectedly human face: the eternal recurrence of calendrical time, the revolution of the seasons, the cycle of days, the constant return of anniversaries and holidays. Certainly, this time is a human time, a time which, as on anniversaries and public holidays, we gladly and voluntarily share with others. This time has legitimate claim to be called our own–and precisely because it is experienced as marginality, as in holidays, evenings, weekends, periods of illness and convalescence, or again as a hiatus between commitments, as moments of discontinuity between phases of experience.

That our own time falls within this natural time is not suprising. For we are, above all, living organisms: our own time is defined by the time during which we are alive. This time, our own time, is (as Freud observed) supervised by the instinct for self-preservation in particular, but also by the psychological principle underlying it whereby people seek out pleasurable rather than disagreeable experiences. Freud argues that the pleasure-principle, like the instinct for self-preservation, is a product of the death instinct. The pleasure principle works to reduce the unsettling intrusions of an inimical social environment; it defends the self from the stressful disruptions brought about by the life-instincts, by the need to create a world in which to live. The pleasure principle, therefore, works to guarantee our own time, by preventing any short-cut to an ultimately inevitable death by ensuring that we instead take ever more complicated, roundabout ways to it ['immer komplizierteren Umwegen bis zur Erreichung des Todeszieles'] so that we can die in our own way and in our own time: so that death comes as the fulfilment of the time of our life.[13]

Certainly, leisure is a way of occupying our own time, but this sense of our own time is granted only by death. What gives leisure its special savour is its disclosure of finitude. For this reason the celebration of anniversaries, the anticipation of our annual holiday, our pleasure at the advent of fixed and movable feasts is not always diminished, but often rather enhanced by the fact that they recur, and with their recurrence mark the passing of time. It would seem, therefore, that such marginal opportunities for leisure as are made available by society, which is inherently competitive and ruthlessly performative, are a grudging condescension to our innate vulnerability. But in any case leisure has always resisted the blandishments of self-transcendance offered by societies fixated with progress or glory. Hence leisure exists even during times in which history and state demand the total sacrifice of self, as in the carol-singing and football games in no-man's-land in the First World War. The exhortations to seize the day [carpe diem], to cultivate one's garden, testify to a fundamental desire in every one of us once and for all to turn our backs on our inscrutable fate, to ignore the weighty issues of the wider world which never go away, and – whatever we mean by it – be ourselves.

Leisure, then, is no narcotic, not a form of escapism, but rather a divergent form of being, a precarious location in time for our own vulnerable preoccupations. When it fufils them, it provides an exhilarating sense of living for its own sake. Like art it proposes 'to give nothing but the highest quality to your moments as they pass, and simply for those moments' sake'.[14] Leisure has the potential to give you the time of your life in those possibly rare moments when, without any sense of hyperbole, you feel you have all the time in the world.

Leisure returns us to our own time; but what corresponding dimension of space does it restore to us? Rilke's poem shows that it provides an alternative place to be in, it provides us with a world of our own. No one recognises the reader, neither the observer who belongs to the routine world, nor even his mother who, if anyone, ought to recognise him. So completely does leisure deprive the person of his daily world that it renders him unrecognisable: his divergent mode of being is unimaginable to anyone who remains in the daily round of things: the divergence is as great as that between the 'serious' adult world and the child's world of make-believe. Hence, as the poem indicates, leisure can to some extent be imposing or arresting; momentarily, at least, it can draw in non-participants. But conversely, so completely does this world of leisure absorb the reader that afterwards it changes entirely his attitude to his ordinary world.

How does leisure grant us a world of our own, a sphere of privacy? And why is it so important? This question implies that, as with time, so with space, little of it can really be called our own. In the kaleidoscope of intentions that represents our social and moral experience, many of the basic shapes are unalterable and the primary colours ineradicable. Asking where our experience of leisure is situated means asking where and how society validates personal interests, and what opportunities it offers for ideas and actions the individual subject considers meaningful. Therefore, defining what sort of an experience leisure is, means enquiring into how we experience the public space in which we live.

'Even the most just, most democratic and most liberal state', Paul Ricoeur argues, 'turns out to be a synthesis of legitimation and violence and has the moral power to make demands and the physical power to coerce.'[15] Modern society is a network of power structures created and sustained by its economic, political and administrative institutions. But these structures are revealed not just in class, economic or social conflicts, but also in a more pervasive social antagonism between individuals, in a sort of 'unsocial sociability' ['ungesellige Geselligkeit'], to use Kant's phrase.[16] No one exists who is not in a position to exert some power over another through his or her social function (from the mechanic who might hold you to ransom if you require his assistance outside working hours to the doctor who might advise you to give up smoking). No one exists who is not in some way the victim of another's political or economic power. Each person has this ambivalent social experience as a function of the social institution to which he or she belongs, in an everyday world where others serve similar institutionalised functions.

Conversely, it is also necessary to emphasise that within the political and economic organisation of a state, structures and processes exist which aim to neutralise opposition and stifle criticism. The result is that society may be divided into those who identify with and promote the interests of their institution and those who do not. That is to say, in every society throughout the world there is a fundamental division 'between those who believe in human omnipotence (who think that everything is possible if one knows how to organize masses for it) and those for whom powerlessness has become the major experience of their lives'.[17] Generally speaking, the bureaucratic structures of state and commercial institutions draw for support on those who not only identify with the real power they exercise, but also need their intimate relationship to this power for the purposes of their own self-transcendence.

Because the social sphere is a force-field of competing political and economic interests from which most people, on account of their inherent powerlessness, are excluded, it is difficult to see how it could also accommodate a world of our own, a space in which we, along with others of a like mind, might say what we want and do as we wish. It is the unequal diffusion of power in society, the lack of control which individuals collectively have over the sheer potentiality they collectively produce, which is personally inhibiting and experientially impoverishing.

The public sphere as the dominion of public opinion now means little more than unstable compromises between the interests of competing institutions and pressure groups. Public tastes can be determined through various forms of disinformation or propaganda. According to Habermas, there has been a reversion to feudal conditions in the public sphere ['eine Art "Refeudalisierung" der Öffentlichkeit']: large organisations compete against each other and the state beyond the gaze of publicity while at the same time resorting to strategies of public relations with the broad mass of the population in order to gain a measure of popular support for their moves. The result is a progressive diminution of the capacity of public opinion to be genuinely critical about the way in which society is managed. Whereas public opinion might once have required decision-makers to be accountable for their actions, now–in the absence of widespread public debate–it is little more than a forum for self-advertisement.[18]

Furthermore, the competition of political and economic interests subverts the very language in which people speak to each other. Man is very much a language animal, language is in truth 'the house of being'. The power struggles of political and economic interests in their perversion of meaning literally take words from our mouth; they are as such a further cause of our cultural impoverishment. The 'all pervasive, rampant degeneration of language in the public sphere' is a major cause of our existential insecurity.[19] Indeed (in the words of Hermann Broch), a veritable 'catastrophe of muteness' ['Katastrophe der Stummheit'] has befallen the public sphere; it is as though the working-person of today has taken a vow of silence more strict than even that of a Trappist monk. He speaks only to come to understandings, in signals, in terms of commercial correspondence. He mentions things that concern him when it is absolutely necessary, but he no longer discusses them.[20]

The sphere of public opinion not only undermines the dignity of human thought by its manipulation of consensus, but also the meaningfulness of human action by its subversion of reality. One of the most important legacies of totalitarianism for governments since the Second World War is the precedents it set for the management of large populations by the manipulation of public information in order to transmute awkward reality into plausible fiction, and baffling coincidences into reassuring consistency.

That reality is inconsistent is a fact of contemporary life, as any news bulletin will confirm. In his novel, *La nausée*, one of the classic descriptions of modern experience, Sartre resorts to a strategy which can be found in other writers of the time such as Döblin, Dos Passos,

Broch or Musil, and which establishes the global situation of the central character. On a cold, windy night, Roquentin, in a bleak moment of realisation, is aware that at that very moment there are liners on the high seas, all bright lights and music, Communists and Nazis skirmishing in Berlin, the unemployed of New York aimlessly walking the pavements, and women putting on make-up before going out for the evening. He knows that each shot ringing out in the Berlin suburb, each convulsion of the wounded, like each careful application of mascara, responds to one or other of his lonely footsteps in the desolate French port.[21]

Few people would deny being familiar with this kind of anxiety. Indeed, everyone has a global imagination of some sort, but what it reveals cannot be reduced to any sense, certainly not to any common sense. And it is precisely for this reason that the lonely individuals of a mass society are vulnerable to manipulation. Unable to bear the accidental, incomprehensible aspects of reality, and so receptive to any kind of sense, however simplistic and misleading, rather than to the world's palpable absurdities, they turn to ideologies to blot out whatever they cannot fathom. 'The masses' escape from reality is a verdict against the world in which they are forced to live and in which they cannot exist, since coincidence has become its supreme master and human beings need the constant transformation of chaotic and accidental conditions into a man-made pattern of relative consistency.'[22] The result, for the individual isolated in the mass, is a complete divorce between the world as it is imagined or received intellectually and the sphere of action, between ordinary experience and predominant interpretations of the world. (A simple example of this is that some people in personal contact with someone visibly of another race can be quite civil, but otherwise can espouse racialist ideas on the basis of what they have read in the newspapers or because of an acquired, yet unreflected prejudice. They may be latent racists or may themselves be victims of a public sphere poisoned by racist ideologies.)

Finally, the public sphere threatens human potentiality. On the one hand, it deprives an individual's life of a sense of possibility. Once the job or the institution takes control of the individual in terms of career structures, pensions, the narrowing down of his or her capacities until they fit those required by the job, the availability of alternatives which he or she might have entertained earlier disappears gradually. Describing the public self-projection of the relatively new class of white-collar technocrats in America, Richard Sennett observes:

The members of this class are subject to institutional definitions of their work which are to a large extent also an institutional definition of their personalities. Against this institutional process, they have few countervailing traditions or artisanal standards; instead, these arrivals to a new class accept the institutional definitions of themselves as valid, and seek to work out patterns of defense and meaning within a situation in which class circumstances and personality are so closely allied. Corporations treat their white-collar technocrats so that . . . the norms of narcissistic absorption are produced; boundaries between self and world are erased because the position at work seems a mirror of personal power; the nature of that power resides, however, not in action, but in potential. The result of this mobilization of narcissism in their lives is that the technical workers' ability to challenge the rules of dominance and discipline which govern their class is destroyed. Class becomes too much a part of themselves to be played with. The mobilization of narcissism by an institution has succeeded in rendering impotent the element of expressive play, that is, play with a remaking of the impersonal rules which govern their actions.[23]

No wonder, then, that the contemporary social landscape seems bleak, with individuals thoroughly assimilated to the institutions which control them manipulated by the terrorising techniques condoned by the performative ethos of modern management, which involve not only the refusal to engage in a discussion of strategies, ends and means, but also the arrogant imposition of its own aims by means of economic threats. What is experienced in this open-air prison of a society, which in its fundamental organisation proclaims its own rigid immutability, is the loss of meaningful futurity. Hence, it seems almost superfluous to add that the historical context of the drastic reduction of the social potential of the individual human being, the nuclear age, contributes its own negating factor in that 'the possibility of our final destruction is, even if this never occurs, the final destruction of our possibilities'.[24]

'Tout ceci nous vise au cerveau': all these reductive tendencies in society culminate in a crisis of morale.[25] Individuals themselves have few defences against the sterility of the public sphere which sooner or later infiltrates and sours their more private concerns. The experiential impoverishment within the public sphere foreshadows a desolate privation. Nothing illustrates this more clearly than the loss of the ideal of personal autonomy during the modern period. The ideal of the autonomous personality which Kant advanced in 1788 in his *Kritik der praktischen Vernunft* as a moral imperative, is regarded by Adorno in 1966 in his essay, 'Glosse über Persönlichkeit', as a matter of reluctant philosophical nostalgia. The autonomous individual is the crux of Kant's philosophy: in it freedom and necessity coincide – freedom from the ignoble servitude to natural instincts, freedom to choose for himself, albeit with the obligation (if only for his own good) to consider and accommodate the interests of other individuals similarly autonomous. It was on this basis that a liberal, enlightened, humane society could be constructed, guaranteed and sustained by a public sphere of opinions formed by proper communication between people. By contrast, Adorno shows how this concept became abused in the course of the nineteenth century to mean now strong or dominant individuals, now absence of definite character (as in television or film personalities produced, he says in *Dialektik der Aufklärung*, like the regular irregularities of Yale locks), now simply eccentricity. In the century and a half since the first formulation of autonomy, all its positive connotations – independence, freedom and rationality – have been erased.[26]

Certainly, with the loss of autonomy and the lack of a public sphere of meaningful speech and action in which to exercise it, the individual is confronted with privacy in its original, classical sense of the deprivation of everything beyond the individual which made life interesting and worthwhile.[27] ('The private man', observes Albert Hirschman, 'used to be found at the bottom of the social scale.'[28]) The development of this impoverishing, personal privation is of a comparatively recent date. Up to the mid-eighteenth century there was a thriving public sphere in which city-dwellers were able to remain strangers to each other even while engaging in social intercourse, because they behaved in accordance with a fairly reliable symbolic code of appearances. It was the emergent bourgeoisie which, in demanding the public accountability of the private personalities of dominant social actors, gradually in the course of the nineteenth century transformed the public sphere into a psychological realm for the interplay of personalities. As power and personality attracted each other, the scope for individual social action diminished. The public transferred its own aspirations to dominant, charismatic figures whom it considered to be personally plausible and itself dwindled to a vast collection of isolated individuals. Even though highly visible to each other, because they lack any recognisable, public conventions which might facilitate meaningful contact, they remain in isolation, wary as they are of exposing their vulnerable, intimate selves to the public gaze.[29]

The individual in his or her isolated privacy experiences a double form of narcissism. One part of it is that in the absence of a truly public sphere, of an opportunity to experience the salutary thrill of foreignness which the encounters with strangers provide, the individual retreats into a realm of ascetic self-interest, or of local, parochial causes which only further inhibit self-knowledge. The other part of it is that this narcissism is self-destructive since, as the case of totalitarianism or of large corporations shows, in the absence of any public sense of self the individual merges his identity by means of a 'compulsive bonding' with the institution on which he depends.[30]

In contemporary society the private realm is a dismal sphere of frustration, boredom and neurosis. The frustration arises from an imbalance between the knowledge people have of what transpires in society, for example by way of the mass-media, and their very limited scope to respond to it by constructive political action. The boredom results from the assimilation of the personality to the institution which sustains it and discloses the ensuing vacuousness of the self, 'We do not like being on our own for long', Ernst Bloch remarks in *Spuren* [Tracks] (1930), his survey of modern cultural attitudes, 'no one can put up with that, having a room of your own is no big deal.' And he adds, 'in ourselves we are still quite empty, we soon drop off if there are no external stimuli. . . . If we cannot get to sleep at night, we are not really awake, we ruminate persistently and corrosively on the same few things ('zähes, verzehrendes Schleichen an Ort und Stelle']. It's then we notice how uncomfortable it is to be totally by ourselves.'[31] In such isolation the individual is left helpless and undefended to confront the irrationality of the world in which he lives. He proceeds through his daily life with all the blind, absurd confidence of a sleepwalker. The neurosis arises with the individual's discontent with the culture he has inherited, from his dismay that for all its ingenuity and control of nature mankind has sacrificed itself to an infernal machine of a society of his own making, and from profound feelings of disorientation because of the disconcerting contradiction between his inner desires and the external world.[32]

In view of the bleakness of this social landscape, there really does appear to be a need to ask if there is a place for leisure in contemporary life. Certainly, leisure has always been a diversion from the rigours of material necessities. Mankind has always had leisure, in the sense that mankind has never just been concerned with satisfying material needs.

Leisure and work are two main dimensions of being which together
constitute the world in which people live. Even so, it is only in the
modern world that leisure seems to be in danger of ceasing to be a
distinct digression from work and becoming ambivalent. Leisure has
been appropriated by an institutionalised, bureaucratic society; both
the state and local government take some responsiblity for promoting
the provision of leisure facilities and activities as a factor in town
planning and social welfare; an extensive and varied leisure industry
has grown up to supply and develop people's requirements for their
spare-time occupations; companies often have their own sports and
leisure organisations with the result, even if not the aim, of reinforcing
work relationships with social contacts; in communist and fascist states
leisure organisations are often adjuncts to social control. But, at the
same time, leisure cannot be entirely appropriated. Even in the most
rigorously organised state there is always some margin of time not
claimed; no life is so thoroughly ordered, since it would be impossible,
except perhaps in a most rigorous prison, for life to be deprived of even
a minimal element of leisure. It is precisely this resistance to social and
political pressures which makes it diverge crucially from the world on
which it depends and enables it to measure the variety of existential
choices and, therefore, the degree of personal meaningfulness society
allows.

  Leisure, then, primarily counteracts the diminution of possibility in
society. Leisure nurtures our interests, it permits us to develop new
interests and new tastes as a form of compensation for the dereliction
of self in the modern world. Hence leisure has an educative function:
our interests and tastes can always be refined and developed if we have
the initiative and invest our own time in them. It, therefore, both
counteracts the impoverishment of experience and restores a sense of
futurity. Admittedly, these interests may be suggested or formulated
by the wider social context which overshadows them, but this does not
detract from the fact that these interests and tastes, however socially
determined, help define us as persons. Here it is inevitably a matter for
social and cultural policy-makers to recognise that the more social and
leisure choices available to a person, the richer and better balanced his
or her life will be. Nevertheless – as is most evident in the case of, say,
model railways or collecting stamps or beer-mats – leisure enables us to
construct even within our social privation meaningful forms of order –
layouts, taxonomies, patterns – over which we have our own
jurisdiction. Consequently, leisure, as an opportunity for self-
discovery, also provides us with occasions for the exercise of personal

autonomy. In all these ways it gives our bereft social selves some content and direction.

But leisure does more than develop for us an enriching privacy; it also helps establish a coherent, even if restricted, public sphere. What enables leisure to institute a realm of public life is the primacy of the common interest which brings people from different walks of life together in specific groups or organisations. For while some leisure interests might be determined by social status or wealth, others – such as music or sport – can transcend these differences. Through such leisure interest groups, the interests and tastes we develop engage the interests and tastes of others – and for the sake of these tastes and interests. These organisations confirm that the development of personal tastes does more than establish the degree of personal autonomy and the freedom needed to form our own judgement. According to Kant, taste judgements, specifically non-utilitarian and formalistic in character, are what permit our subjective viewpoint to be generally valid since they presuppose in others a faculty of appreciation similar to our own (as when, for example, two football supporters of opposing teams can concur on the technical and formal merits of the match in question, regardless of which side won). Hence, while losing none of its subjective value, our taste participates in a consensus, helps constitute a community of opinion which itself encourages the social cohesion of a public sphere of interests. Indeed, as Kant also argues, the subjective generalities of taste judgements presuppose a social forum in which they can be discussed, if they are to flourish. In this way, even in an inclement historical situation, they help constitute an independent sphere of legitimate human interests.[33]

Certainly, in leisure interest groups which provide a public forum for private tastes, there is a reflection of the Enlightenment, a sociable period if ever there was one, in which the balance between common interests and public order was maintained by numerous clubs, philosophical and natural history societies, as well as in the coffee-house or in the aristocratic salon.[34] Voluntary leisure organisations, as self-regulating bodies, perhaps create something analagous to a collectively governed republic, which for many Enlightenment philosophers was the ideal political form.

Lastly, by means of such voluntary organisations leisure helps re-establish the specificities of the spoken word. Here policies and directions can be meaningfully discussed by all those concerned. In this connection, however insignificant an individual's routine social status, he or she can, if so inclined, rise to hold an office in the group or club which organises his or her leisure interest. Thus leisure provides new personae for us to adopt and also a stage on which to try them out. For here – as Kant also argued – whatever their scope for self-expression at their place of work, people can make use of their own understanding and judgement in a forum where their opinions are likely to carry. Here too runs the writ of Locke's law of opinion or reputation which exerts a beneficial influence through peoples' sensitivity to the moral and social conventions of their peers.[35] Here too there is confirmation of Karl Jaspers' conviction that a free society of independent, rational human beings both presupposes and requires for its future survival genuine discussion and communication amongst its members. For, according to Jaspers, man in isolation is an absurdity; man can only become truly human in conjunction with others by means of communication.[36]

Leisure, therefore, restores to the public sphere an aesthetic dimension, a means and an occasion for being different from one's routine self, which it had generally lacked since the nineteenth century.[37] This is even true in the case of the 'stringent selfishness' of reading, even if the community of interest it establishes is more abstract – a community of reason and imagination, a republic of letters crossing space and time, a forum for a never-ending discussion of interests and tastes in which individuals from different cultures may meet, and to which they may variously contribute. 'Books', observed the novelist Jean Paul in 1807, 'establish a universal republic, a federation of nations or a Jesuit society in the best sense or a human society by virtue of which a second or duplicate Europe arises which like London spans several counties and parishes.'[38]

Nevertheless, for all its benefits, there is no point in pretending that leisure can compensate totally for a dismal social world. Although I have described leisure as an alternative way of being, I would not wish to imply that leisure is man's sole, authentic mode of being. For one thing, to label contemporary society as inauthentic does nothing to diminish its claustrophobia and its real inimical character. For another, leisure itself can only be a provisional substitute for the lack of properly free and open political and economic institutions, for a truly tolerant public sphere. Just what is man's authentic being is perhaps almost impossible to say. Regrettably, it is surely indefensible to maintain with humanism that there is a resilient human spirit which inspires liberal, enlightened values. But there is also no reason to believe either that each individual is just a product of historical circumstances, that 'man has no nature–what he has instead is history'.[39] If that were the case, we would probably, in the contemporary state of things, be hardly aware that we are entitled to leisure as a basic existential digression.

Rather, the assumption underlying this argument is that there exists in each individual what Freud called an 'invincible core of nature' ['ein Stück der unbesiegbaren Natur'] which is a foundation for historical accretions of socialisation and acculturation. This residue of nature may well appear to be a liability since it frustrates mankind's attempts at self transcendance through material progress. But this resistance of nature is not such a bad thing, and Kant was surely not entirely justified in defining personality in terms of a purely moral independence from its demands. For if it prevents culture from being all-powerful and all-embracing, it also prevents individuals from becoming infinitely and helplessly manipulable. It is this biological residue which prompts the demand for leisure, since, in its unreflected reaction to excessive social intrusion, it posits intuitively the possibility of a world more conducive to the living of a life of our own than the present, overdetermined world. This, then is the way in which leisure compensates for individual privation. It is the free response of ordinary people to the organised loneliness of their lives and, within its modest limits, ensures them a degree of happiness.[40] In this sense, it is like a solitary candle in a room during a winter's night; it cannot shed much light or heat but at least, as long as it lasts, it wards off the frost and the absolute dark.

Specifying the location of leisure within the sphere of everyday experience enables us to answer our original question about the point of leisure and the nature of the experiences it offers. Leisure is truly an alternative way of being. Like Rilke's reader, when we are at leisure, when we do things in our own time and in our own space, we leave our everyday existence for another way of being. Conversely, when we return to it, we return as strangers. But in what way is leisure divergent? Are there not good grounds for qualifying much of what has been said by saying simply that if leisure is an alternative, it is an alternative which does not lie very far beyond the world of work, but rather runs parallel with it, often very closely parallel? For example, what is the difference between the professional cabinet-maker and the office-or factory-worker who is a skilled and experienced woodworker; between the tailoress or craftswoman who sells hand-made dresses and a working woman who makes her own clothes; or between the professional actress and the star of an amateur dramatic society's play? In general, there is hardly any leisure activity which does not have an economically or politically motivated, or socially necessary or functioning couterpart. Leisure activities can, however, be more stressful or dangerous than work (particularly hazardous sports, for example); but they can also be far less stressful: as in the case of holiday-makers who spend most of their time sunbathing, or even simply sightseeing, just travelling as they please and simply looking at what is there.

The only dimension which can accommodate such a multifarious phenomenon as leisure is the aesthetic. Leisure is a diversion of our being into the aesthetic dimension; in the midst of ordinary life it makes aesthetic experiences widely accessible. A phenomenology of leisure as an aesthetic experience must surely include the following elements. It is, in the first instance, strictly mimetic, hence its parallelism with the world of work. Leisure is mimetic since human experience and culture are specifically motivated by mimesis – as Aristotle argued: 'The instinct for imitation is inherent in man from his earliest days; he differs from other animals in that he is the most imitative of creatures, and he learns his lessons by imitation. Also inborn in all of us is the instinct to enjoy works of imitation.' And in the case of leisure the mimetic medium is not just human action, as in the case of drama, but indeed existence itself. The world of leisure does, therefore, run very closely parallel with the world of work, but as an alternative mode of existence. It is, therefore, complete in itself, autonomous within its own sphere, an imaginary repository of other ways of being, set in a time which is not our routine time, a spatial dimension which is not our routine space, a momentary escape from our historical fate, and a necessary means of reasserting humane priorities in a society inimical to them.[41]

But with leisure as with all good imitations, it is often difficult to tell the original from the copy. In these cases, though, whichever is the original or the copy, it is sufficient that the duplication permits another way of being to exist. For example, the man whose hobby is gardening has surely skills and aims similar to the man who earns his living as a gardner; both the professional and the amateur dressmaker are under an obligation as much to the customer as to themselves to get the look of the dress right so that it can pass muster in public. Certainly, this is also a question pertinent to the entertainment industry in which people, the stars, make a living out of imitating natural human skills; for example, singing or cookery demonstrations. The problem is analysed in an ironical way in Kafka's story, 'Josefine, die Sängerin oder das Volk der Mäuse'. Josefine's song is entrancingly powerful even though the mice listening to her (says the narrator) are too care-worn and have too hard a life to appreciate something as remote from and elevated above their existence as music. But in trying to discern the source of the power of Josefine's singing the narrator comes to doubt whether she in fact sings at all, but simply squeaks, which is of course something mice do all the time and so it could hardly be called the virtuoso art form Josefine claims it to be. In the end, he concludes that it is the force of her personality which enthrals them and makes them admire in her what they do not admire in themselves.[42]

Leisure also, as Rilke's poem suggests, satisfies a human need for play, for pretence, for rehearsing emotions and situations not granted in the daily run of things. Play breaks the hold on us of the given realities of our lives: it holds up to us a mirror in which we see ourselves reflected as we are; it enables us to countenance another world in which to be and helps persuade us of the fortuitousness of the reality in which we ordinarily exist.[43]

Leisure is also non-performative in terms of reigning socio-economic norms. Certainly many leisure activities have to be performed, but the unimpeachable quality of the performance may well come secondary to the pleasure which it provides to the performers and even to their often indulgent audience of friends and acquaintances. Mastering the techniques of playing in a string quartet may well be difficult, but an amateur group performing for a good cause amongst friends is bound to be forgiven any dissonances or faults of timing which might occur since the audience in any case takes pleasure in their pleasure and supports the cause the players themselves are supporting. In other words, leisure does not add to the world which is ready-made and full ['die fertig-volle Welt'], a world already claustrophobically finite, a world in which more has happened than we know ['Mehr als wir erfuhren ist geschehen']. Leisure clears what Rilke calls a 'pure space in existence' for us.[44]

Lastly, leisure is non-transcendental. The activities, the experiences, the interests are valued for themselves and for the fact that they happen in our own time and space. They serve no ends of society beyond themselves. The most radical expression of this non-transcendental quality of leisure is when one decides to do nothing, to relax entirely, or simply to see the sights. For this reason, Adorno is wrong when he sees sunbathing, the tanning of the skin, as extending to the person the Marxist notion of the fetish-character of consumer goods. To treat ourselves as an object is to bring about a depletion of the power of the state which already treats us as objects; the voluntary action of our self-reduction, of putting our will in abeyance, is what brings about the depletion. More than that, it is a radical expression of a desire to do nothing, of a refusal to be taken in by the state's treacherous desire for human self-transcendence through material progress.[45]

Leisure, then, gives access to the aesthetic dimension of life. As the demands of history and society become more rigorous, the only dimensions available for human interest, the only means of expression of hopes and dreams of rediscovering everything that society itself discards, is the aesthetic dimension, serious yet subversively non-committal, non-productive, non-performative. Art redeems ordinary experience. Leisure is art of a second degree. We may not be able to write dramas, the opportunities for play may have receded from our lives, we may envy the consistency of significant public figures. But leisure provides the opportunities for us to be actors in a scenario of our own choosing. The formal structures of leisure, like the formal structures of the work of art, lift us out of the routine public sphere into a private yet common human world of meaningfulness.

Leisure is valuable, even though it is marginal, because it enables us to conjecture a way we would like to be, another way of being, but a way in which we can never totally be. An image, that of a reader, introduced this idea; and the best way of showing how this other way of being, which leisure affords, is experienced, is to draw on another image, this time from the history of art: Chardin's picture of a young man blowing bubbles, entitled 'The Soap Bubble' (1731–3).[46]

The young man in question is in the middle of the picture and claims our attention: the eye travels along the straw to the huge bubble. To his right stands a glass of soap and water; to his left a smaller face stares apparently wide-eyed in admiration. The glass, the young man and the face are doubly framed: once by the frame of the painting itself, once by the window aperture. But the bubble is suspended between the two: within our frame and so beyond our mundane world, but outside their frame and beyond their world. Behind the young man the room in which they live is in darkness: the space into which he leans in this idle moment is bright – and the brightest object in this elusive, aesthetic space is the bubble. Other bright elements are the glass and soap solution on the ledge, on the margins of the two spheres of experience (since the material world is common to both necessity and leisure) like the upper part of the young man's body and, to a lesser extent, the face looking out from within the darkened room.

This painting symbolically recapitulates the notion of leisure as an alternative way of being. The window is for contemplating; like sight-seeing it induces in the individual an aesthetic frame of mind. The young man turns his back on the dark mundane world, but he does not look out or at us. But rather from the mundane objects of his routine world: glass, soap, straw, items from a contingent world, but items nevertheless which will outlast him, he produces a bubble – at once the most dispensable, fragile, negligent thing in this world and yet still a thing which is whole, formally harmonious and pleasing, and endowed with a tremulous perfection. Though the bubble (like the house of cards or the game of knuckle-bones in other paintings by Chardin) may be regarded as a conventional symbol of vanity, that does not disqualify it from being an image of leisure. If we understand vanity as futility, then the futility of leisure is in itself a protest against the insane desire for self-transcendence through progress and history. If vanity is understood as gratuitous and idle self-regard, as absorption in our own appearance, then leisure is also valuable in that it reaffirms our presence whereas society itself conspires ultimately to suppress us.

But the bubble has also a deeper, philosophical meaning as these words of Pope, Chardin's contemporary, suggest:

> Oh blindness to the future! kindly giv'n,
> That each may fill the circle mark'd by heav'n;
> Who sees with equal eye, as God of all,
> A hero perish, or a sparrow fall,
> Atoms or systems into ruin hurl'd,
> And now a bubble burst, and now a world.[47]

That a bubble can represent a world is an idea which derives from Plato's *Timaeus*, in which the cosmos is defined as a sphere because that is 'the fitting shape' which 'comprises within itself all the shapes there are' and, because 'equidistant in all directions from the centre of the extremities' it is 'of all shapes . . . the most perfect and the most self-similar'.[48] Therefore, the bubble symbolises an aesthetic moment which discloses a truth and perfection beyond mundane reality – and shared also by the younger person who looks on in wonderment. Suspended not in any routine space or time but in an elusive aesthetic dimension, the bubble represents the ideal of a way to be, an ideal which can only be disclosed when we, like the two figures in the painting, are at our leisure. Hence this image provides a clue for its ultimate significance: that if, as Stendhal said, beauty is a promise of happiness, then leisure is surely a brief glimpse of Utopia.

Notes

1. Martin Heidegger, 'Wozu Dichter?' (1926), in *Holzwege,* 5th edn (Frankfurt am Main, 1972) p. 249; G. W. F. Hegel, *Vorlesungen über die Philosophie der Geschichte* (1837), in *Sämtliche Werke, Jubiläumsausgabe,* 20 vols. ed. Hermann Glockner, 4th edn (Stuttgart, 1961) vol. xi, pp. 44, 92, 110.
2. Rainer Maria Rilke, *Sämtliche Werke,* ed. Ruth Sieber-Rilke and Ernst Zinn, 6 vols (Frankfurt am Main, 1955–66) vol. i, pp. 636–7. The English prose version is my own.
3. Theodor W. Adorno, 'Freizeit' (1969), in *Stichworte Kritische Modelle 2,* 3rd edn (Frankfurt am Main, 1972) pp. 57–67.
4. George Steiner, 'Text and Context', in *On Difficulty and Other Essays* (Oxford, 1978) p. 10.
5. Immanuel Kant, *Kritik der reinen Vernunft* (1787), in *Gesammelte Schriften,* ed. Akademie der Wissenschaften der DDR, 29 vols (Berlin, 1966–75) vol. iii, p. 51ff.
6. Ernst Bloch, *Erbschaft dieser Zeit* (1935) (Frankfurt am Main, 1972) pp. 68, 104ff.
7. Theodor W. Adorno, *Minima Moralia. Reflexionen aus dem beschädigten Leben* (1951) (Frankfurt am Main, 1978) p. 39; Hannah Arendt, *The Origins of Totalitarianism* (1951; reprint ed. London, 1986) pp. 332–3.
8. Immanuel Kant, 'Idee zu einer allgemeinen Geschichte in weltbürgerlicher Absicht' (1784), in *Gesammelte Schriften,* vol. viii, pp. 30–l.
9. Jean-Paul Sartre, *Plaidoyer pour les intellectuels* (Paris, 1972) pp. 49–50.
10. Paul Valéry, 'Notes sur la grandeur et la décadence de l'Europe' (1927), in *Regards sur le monde actuel,* in *Oeuvres,* ed. Jean Hytier, 2 vols (Paris, 1962) vol. ii, pp. 929–34.
11. Charles Péguy, *Clio, Dialogue de l'histoire et de l'âme paienne,* in *Oeuvres en prose, 1901–1914,* ed. Marcel Peguy (Paris, 1961) pp. 130–1.
12. Paul Valéry, 'Propos sur le progrès' (1929), in *Regards sur le monde actuel,* in vol. ii, pp. 1022–7; Max Weber, *Wissenschaft als beruf* (1919), in *Gesammelte Aufsätze zur Wissenschaftslehre,* ed. J. Winckelmann, 3rd edn (Tübingen, 1968) pp. 594–5.
13. Sigmund Freud, 'Jenseits des Lustprinzips' (1920), in *Das Ich und das Es und andere metapsychologische Schriften* (Frankfurt am Main, 1982) pp. 148–9, 168–9.
14. Walter Pater, *The Renaissance* (1873), with an introduction and notes by Kenneth Clark (London, 1971) p. 224.
15. Paul Ricoeur, 'État et violence' (1957), in *Histoire et vérité,* 3rd edn (Paris, 1964) p. 247.
16. Kant 'Idee zu einer allgemeinen Geschichte in weltbürgerlicher Absicht' vol. viii, p. 20.
17. Arendt, *The Origins of Totalitarianism,* p. vii.
18. Jürgen Habermas, 'Öffentlichkeit' (1964), in *Kultur und Kritik, Verstreute Aufsätze,* 2nd edn (Frankfurt am Main, 1977) pp. 67–8.
19. Martin Heidegger, 'Brief über den Humanismus' (1946), in *Wegmarken,* 2nd edn (Frankfurt am Main, 1978) pp. 315–16.
20. Hermann Broch, 'Über die Grundlagen des Romans *Die Schlafwandler*'

(1931), in *Kommentierte Werkausgabe*, ed. Paul Michael Lützeler, 13 vols (Frankfurt am Main, 1978–1981) vol. I, pp. 728–33.

21. Jean-Paul Sartre, *La Nausée* (1938), in *Oeuvres romanesques*, ed. Michel Contat and Michel Rybalka (Paris, 1981) p. 67.

22. Arendt, *The Origins of Totalitarianism*, p. 352.

23. Richard Sennett, *The Fall of Public Man*, (London, 1986) p. 328.

24. Theodor W. Adorno, 'Kulturkritik und Gesellschaft' (1949), in *Prismen Kulturkritik und Gesellschaft* (1955; Frankfurt am Main, 1976) p. 30; Jean-Francois Lyotard, *La Condition postmoderne* (Paris, 1979) pp.102–3; epigraph to Günther Anders, *Die atomare Drohung. Radikale überlegungen*, 5th edn (Munich, 1986).

25. Paul Valéry, 'Fluctuations sur la liberté' (1938), in *Regards sur le monde actuel*, vol. II, pp. 968–9.

26. Immanuel Kant, *Kritik der praktischen vernunft* (1788), in *Gesammelte Schriften*, vol. II, pp. 71ff.; Theodor W. Adorno 'Glosse über Persönlichkeit' (1966), in *Stichworte*, pp. 51–6; Max Horkheimer and Theodor W. Adorno, *Dialektik der Aufklärung* (1947; Frankfurt am Main, 1973) p. 139.

27. Hannah Arendt, *The Human Condition* (Chicago, 1958) p. 38.

28. Albert Hirschman, *Shifting Involvements: Private Interest and Public Action* (Oxford, 1985) pp. 121–2.

29. Sennett, *The Fall of Public Man*, passim.

30. Ibid., p. 259 ff.

31. Ernst Bloch, *Spuren* (1930; Frankfurt am Main, 1969) p. 11.

32. Hermann Broch, 'Der Roman *Die Schlafwandler*', in *Kommentierte Werkausgabe*, vol. I. p. 719; Sigmund Freud, *Das Unbehagen in der Kultur* (1930), in *Abriss der Psychoanalyse. Das Unbehagen in der Kultur* (Frankfurt am Main, 1977) p. 87; Friedrich Nietzsche, 'Vom Nutzen und Nachteil der Historie für das Leben' (1874) in *Unzeitgemässe Betrachtungen*, in *Werke*, ed. Karl Schlechta, 3 vols (Munich, 1954–6) vol. I, p. 232.

33. Immanuel Kant, *Kritik der Urteilskraft* (1790), in *Gesammelte Schriften*, vol. V, pp. 201–356.

34. Richard van Dülmen, *Die Gesellschaft der Aufklärer. Zur bürgerlichen Emanzipation und aufklärerischen Kultur in Deutschland* (Frankfurt am Main, 1986) pp. 120 ff.

35. Immanuel Kant, 'Beantwortung der Frage: Was ist Aufklärung?', in *Gesammelte Schriften*, pp. 33–42; John Locke, *An Essay Concerning Human Understanding* (1690), ed. John Yolton, 2 vols (London, 1967) pp. 296–30.

36. Karl Jaspers, *Vernunft und Existenz. Fünf Vorlesungen* (1935; Munich, 1973) pp. 70 ff.; 'Über meine Philosphie' (1941), in *Rechenschaft und Ausblick, Reden und Aufsätze* (Munich,1958) pp. 415 ff.

37. Sennett, *The Fall of Public Man*, pp. 28–9, 259 ff., 313 ff. My concept of leisure is conceived, partially at least, as a response to Sennett's argument that the 'aesthetic dimension in everyday life gradually withered. It was replaced by a society in which formal art accomplished tasks of expression which were difficult or impossible to accomplish in ordinary life' (p. 313).

38. Jean Paul Friedrich Richter, *Levana oder Erziehlehre* (1807), in *Sämtliche Werke*, ed. Norbert Miller, 10 vols (Munich. 1967) vol. v, p. 550.

39. J. Ortega y Gasset, 'History as System', in *Philosophy and History, Essays Presented to Ernst Cassirer,* ed. R. Klibansky and H. J. Paton (Gloucester, Mass., 1975) pp. 312–13.

40. Sigmund Freud, *Das Unbehagen in der Kultur*, in *Das Ichund des Es und andere metapsychologische Schriften*, p. 83; Lionel Trilling, 'Freud: Within and Beyond Culture' (1955), in *Beyond Culture, Essays on Literature and Learning* (Harmondsworth, Middx, 1967) p. 106; Arendt, *The Origins of Totalitarianism*, pp. 474–9.

41. Aristotle, *On the Art of Poetry*, in *Classical Literary Criticism*, trans. with an introduction by T. S. Dorsch (Harmondworth, Middx, 1965) p. 35; André Malraux, *L'Homme précaire et la littérature* (Paris, 1977) pp. 159, 196, 274.

42. Franz Kafka, 'Josefine, die Sängerin oder das Volk der Mäuse' (1924), in *Sämtliche Erzählungen*, ed. Paul Raabe (Frankfurt am Main, 1983) p. 173.

43. Friedrich Schiller, 'Über die ästhetische Erziehung des Menschen' (1795), in *Sämtliche Werke*, ed. G. Fricke and H. G. Göpfert, 5 vols (Munich, 1958–9) vol. v, pp. 657–8. See also Herbert Marcuse, 'Über den affirmativen Charakter der Kultur' (1937), in *Kultur und Gesellschaft*, 2 vols (Frankfurt am Main, 1973) vol. i, pp. 82 ff.

44. Paul Valéry, 'Avant-Propos' to *Regards sur le monde actuel*, in *Oeuvres*, vol. ii, p. 923, and 'Le temps du monde fini commence'; Rainer Maria Rilke, 'Sonnett' (1922), in *Werke*, vol. ii, pp. 135–6; and *Duineser Elegien* (1921–2), ibid., vol. i, p. 724; 'Wir haben nie, nicht einen einzigen Tag, / den reinen Raum vor uns, in den die Blumen / unendlich aufgehn' (viii. Elegy).

45. Agnes Heller, 'Enlightenment Against Fundamentalism', *New German Critique*, vol. 23 (1981) pp. 13–26. But see also Wolfgang Hildesheimer's short story, '1956 – ein Pilzjahr', in *Lieblose Legenden* (Frankfurt am Main, 1972) pp. 21–34. The (fictional) Pilz, allegedly the pioneer of sunbathing, devoted his life to dissuading his Romantic contemporaries from creating their immortal works.

46. Georges Wildenstein, *Chardin*, revised and enlarged by Daniel Wildenstein (Oxford, 1969) pp. 157–8.

47. Alexander Pope, *An Essay on Man* (1733–4), in *Poetical Works*, ed. Herbert Davis (Oxford, 1983) p. 243.

48. Plato, *Timaeus*, in *Timaeus, Critias, Cleitophon, Menexenus, Epistles*, trans. R. G. Bury (London, 1966). See also Leonardo Olschki, 'Der geometrische Geist in Literatur und Kunst', *Deutsche Vierteljahesschrift für Literaturwissenschaft und Geistesgeschichte*, vol. 8 (1930) pp. 521–4.

7

Sport as Moral Educator: Reason and Habit on the School Playing Field

SIMON EASSOM

Many of us believe that sport is more than just the education of the physical. Or rather, it *should* be more than just this. Many claims have been made for the varied functions of physical education and participation in sport. Most of these link, in some way, the situations encountered in sport with those of everyday life. Sport can be considered as a training ground.

Some of these links are immediately obvious: the competitive nature of sport is a preparation for a competitive society; fair play in sport is congruent with the notion of social justice;[1] team sports promote an altruistic orientation that is desirable in a co-operative environment; and most obvious of all, physical activity helps to develop a fit and healthy body that is needed to cope with the stresses and rigours of life.[2] Yet, the identification of these links merely illustrates commonalities and does not necessarily entail anything carried over from one to the other. The further claim, that sport *can* serve the purpose of the developing socially orientated qualities in its participants, has been made. Peter Arnold has prescribed to this view:

> One of the main concerns of education is the development of character and it is only right that it should interest itself in the direction it should take. The following socially orientated qualities should be fostered: kindliness, unselfishness, friendliness, truthfulness, courtesy, helpfulness, tolerance, cheerfulness, loyalty, co-operation and a general consideration for others.[3]

Views such as this are based on the 'links' mentioned above, and accept that sport offers numerous opportunities for concomitant learnings. For example, a child participating in a group activity is in a situation where he or she must be: (a) considerate or inconsiderate of others, (b) selfish or unselfish, (c) tolerant or intolerant, (d) reliable or unreliable, (e) fair or unfair, and (f) self-controlled or lacking in self-control.These situations clearly permit dual possibilities, but the teacher should in some way bring out the 'good' qualities. (we shall only indirectly consider, at a later point in the discussion, whether this is achievable or not.) This is often attempted covertly as part of what is known as the 'hidden curriculum'. That is, these things are not openly taught, but are realised through a child's overall immersion in the educational institution. The child is able to 'practise' the roles and develop standards of behaviour that are expected by society in general. Supposedly, the earlier a child is orientated towards a desirable code of conduct, the more internal the controls upon him or her become.

Physical education provides many decision-provoking situations through which a child can habitualise desirable behaviour. Arnold illustrates this,

> The activities with which physical education is concerned call for real decisions in real situations. They are not hypothetical, they are actual. The touch-judge whose team is drawing and who sees a winger of his team score a try after he has put his foot in touch is left with a choice of whether or not to put up his flag. He must make a decision and he will be forced into a position of acting truthfully or untruthfully. It is hoped he will make the right choice, in keeping with what he knows to be correct. It is no academic nuance. It is a test case of practical application.[5]

Most school sports and games played at a recreational level provide a variety of situations such as this. In our friendly tennis matches, there are no line judges or umpires. When we climb, there is nobody there to see if we pull on the rope. And golf especially is a game where moral conduct and etiquette are fundamental to the activity, yet it is a game that gives more opportunities to cheat than any other.

ORIGINS OF THE RELATIONSHIP BETWEEN SPORT AND MORAL EDUCATION

Among the middle and upper classes in the nineteen century, such games as golf, cricket and tennis appealed to the desire (associated with protestantism) to test one's character. The strict adherence to the ethics of the game was a distinguishing feature of the 'gentleman amateur' who was concerned with 'playing the game' and not merely winning at all costs. Most of the claims for the character-building and friendship-forming aspects of sport arise from this era: a period in which a sharp distinction was first made between amateur and professional; when many team games were formalised and regulated; and when a philosophy of athleticism evolved that became known as 'muscular Christianity'. Redmond summarises some of the tenets of this philosophy.

> The sentiments of the muscular Christian gospel [were] that physical activity and sports (especially team games like cricket and football) contributed towards the development of moral character, fostered a desirable patriotism and that such participation and its ensuing virtues were transferable to other situations and/or later life (such as from playground to battlefield).[6]

As Redmond points out, the principal sports believed to help develop desirable virtues were team games. These embodied the spirit of unselfishness and taught respect for others. This is not to deny that the Victorians played to win. They were tough and aggressive competitors. But victory could not be gained at the expense of attendance to the constitutive rules and those of 'gentlemanly conduct'. The desire to win was definitely the motivation for taking part, although it could not be separated from how the game was played. These aspects simply added to the character-building attributes of team games. Defeat helped to develop courage and perseverance. It also tied together the players in harmonious effort and led to a respectful appreciation of the opponent's victorious struggle. Charles Kingsley, whose work was some of the earliest to be labelled as 'muscular Christianity', wrote in his *Health and Education* (1874):

> That games conduce, not merely to physical but to moral health; that in the playing fields boys acquire virtues which no books can give them; not merely daring and endurance, but, better still, temper, self restraint, fairness, honour, unenvious approbation of anothers success, and all that 'give and take' of life which stand a man in good stead when he goes forth into the world, and without which, indeed his success is always marred and partial.[7]

These games were often played without referees or umpires. Indeed, when the Football Association introduced the penalty kick (in 1891) for an intentional foul in front of the goal, many former public school players were offended by the suggestion that one gentleman would intentionally foul another.[8] Similarly, the law introduced by the Association in 1880 to penalise 'ungentlemanly conduct' was designed to prevent a breach of the very class-conscious social mores.

The imposition of both these laws and others took place at the same time as professionalism in sport began to increase. The moral conceptions of sport began to differ when it was used for utilitarian purposes. The ideal of fair play, prevalent amongst those who considered sport as a hobby or leisure activity, was left behind by the priority of team interest and desire for victory. Once a referee or umpire was introduced, the notion of cheating began to change from simply breaking the rules to breaking the rules with the intention of deceiving the umpire. Overt breaking of the rules became acceptable. The referee was there to penalise this, which made the offence condonable. The players openly accepted the eye-for-an-eye orientation of offence and penalty.

Whereas moral conduct in team games began to alter from the 'gentlemanly', act-orientated codes of the amateur to the utilitarian rule orientated codes of the professional, the opposite shift took place in mountaineering. In fact, rock-climbing (as distinct from mountaineering) evolved out of this shift.

The Development of Mountaineering as a Sport

The so-called 'Golden Age' of mountaineering refers to the nine-or ten-year period between 1856 and 1865 when mountain climbing evolved as a sport. Up until the late eighteenth century, few people attempted to climb the fearful mountains of the European Alps. Indeed, they were seen 'horrid' or 'awful', in the Gothic sense of these words. Those who did were either scientists or from military backgrounds; if not, they were tempted by reward or fame. Initially then, the mountains were objects of utility.

The first major conquest, that of Mont Blanc (the highest mountain in Western Europe), illustrates this. The two successful climbers are exemplary of the early adventurers. Dr Michel-Gabriel Paccard's principal interest in reaching the summit was to prove that Mont Blanc was higher than the (then) generally accepted height of 4,777m. (it is actually 4,807m.). He formed an unusual partnership with the unpopular guide Jacques Balmat. Balmat was solely motivated by the substantial prize money offered by the distinguished professor from Geneva, Honoré Benedict de Saussure. In 1760, de Saussure attempted to scale the mountain to make scientific investigations. Unsuccessful, he offered a reward to anyone who could find a way to the summit that he might follow. Balmat was so intent on gaining this prize that he left his mortally ill daughter in order to make an attempt (which failed). She died while he was on the mountain. It was not until 1786 that the ascent was finally made.[9]

In the next fifty years, the mountains were visited more frequently, often by local mountaineers who undertook their ascents for the sake of climbing itself. The great impetus to the spreading of this interest amongst the British came from the writings of John Ruskin (1819–1900). Ruskin changed the 'dreadful' image of the mountains into one of romance and even mysticism. The culmination of this growing interest was Alfred Willis's ascent of the Wetterhorn in 1854. He described the ascent in his widely published *Wanderings Among the High Alps*. From here on, mountaineering became firmly established as a sport. Within three years (1857), the exclusive British Alpine Club was formed and the sport was pursued with such enthusiasm that by the end of the 1865 season nearly every major Alpine peak had been scaled.

This enthusiasm was almost exclusively British and dominated by the middle and upper classes. This is evident from the fact that it was not until 1863 that the Swiss formed an Alpine Club. The German and French clubs were not formed until 1869 and 1874, respectively. At the same time, the stigma of professionalism hung over climbing for utilitarian purposes. For this reason, climbs were always 'guided' by local experts, even though many of the British mountaineers became equal in knowledge and experience. This was purely a hobby-like activity for the 'gentleman amateur'.

The 'Golden Age' ended in 1865 with the ascent of the last major peak, the Matterhorn (also the scene of the first major tragedy). In 1860, Edward Whymper first arrived in Zermatt as an artist, but became compelled to climb by the desire to conquer the unscaled Weisshorn. When he was beaten to this by John Tyndall and company, he turned his attention to the Matterhorn.[10] On 14 July 1865, Whymper reached the summit with two guides and four other fellow climbers. On the descent, the youngest and least experienced member of the party, Douglas Hadow, slipped and pulled three others with him to their deaths. Only the poor quality of the rope between these four and the others, which broke, prevented them from being dragged down also. Success and tragedy made Whymper the most well-known climber in the world, and his first book, *Scrambles Amongst the Alps, 1860–9*, became a bestseller. A passage from the book sums up what the Victorians felt about their pastime. It is interestingly comparable to the writings of Kingsley and Hughes,

> We glory in the physical regeneration which is the product of our exertions; we exult over the grandeur of the scenes that are brought before our eyes, the splendours of sunrise and sunset, and the beauties of hill, dale, lake, wood and waterfall; but we value more highly the development of manliness, and the evolution, under combat with difficulties, of those noble qualities of human nature – courage, patience, endurance and fortitude.[11]

The interest in climbing for its own sake was reflected by the development of rock climbing as a separate pursuit. No lofty peaks were attained, nor glory gained for summits conquered. People began to climb for the sake of climbing. Rock-climbing thus evolved in the Lake Distrct of England and the Snowdon area of North Wales between the 1870s and the 1890s. It was the creation of a small group of people who shared three main qualities, as Hankinson notes, 'a zest for sport, a high level of culture and education, and a uniquely romantic attitude'.[12] This romantic attitude was expressed in the poetry of William Wordsworth (himself a Lakelander), a century before.

>   And I have felt
> A presence that disturbs me with joy
> Of elevated thoughts, a sense sublime
> Of something far more deeply interfused
> Whose dwelling is the light of setting suns,
> And the round ocean and the living air,
> And the blue sky, and the mind of man,
> A motion and a spirit, that impels
> All thinking things, and objects of all thought,
> And rolls through all things. Therefore I am still
> A lover of the meadows and the woods,
> And mountains . . .[13]

This romantic frame of mind continued amongst the early climbers, and the growing circle of participants became as much a social group as a climbing one.

EVOLUTION AND ACCEPTANCE OF SPORT'S INHERENT VALUES

The writings of the Romantic 'Trust' in the early part of the twentieth century emphasised the social interaction and companionship found in the sport of climbing. This was enhanced by the symbolic importance of the rope. The rope, tied around each climber's waist and knotted at the front, signified the epitome of dependence: the 'umbilical cord'.[14] The relationship between the two climbers was realised in the mutual dependence of each on the other. This basis of comradeship became known as the 'kinship of the rope': 'Each roped man deliberately places his life in the hands of his companion. . . . After many or arduous climbs together, individuals feel deeply this kinship of the rope.'[15] The 'kinship' was at first a negative dependence. The ropes and protection techniques were so unreliable that a climber could not risk falling. This was likely to be disastrous for both members of the rope. With the advent of better protection this dependence became positive: a member of the party could now rely on being held in the case of a slip.

The Outward Bound Movement and Beyond

The virtuous benefits of climbing were accepted openly by the Outward Bound movement. Its original founder, Kurt Hahn, made limited claims for these benefits. He proposed that the physical challenges of the outdoors could lead to an awareness of dormant capacities within ourselves. But this did not prevent others from exaggerating the claims. Munrow mentions some of these:

> Some early brochures from Outward Bound Schools were fairly liberally besprinkled with the phrases such as 'self-reliance', ' moral stamina', 'initiative' and 'powers of leadership'; one described courses as a splendid bridge to any career' and as enabling 'any boy to meet the responsibilities of manhood with greater understanding and confidence'.[16]

Not only have the claims remained, but others have been added. Outward Bound courses have become tailored especially for management training. Donnelly illustrates how, in the late 1960s and early 1970s, business magazines, such as *News Front: Management's News Magazine* and *Business Week* were publishing articles on

'Summer Camps with a Difference' and 'Pitting Managers Against Nature', which stated 'We look to Outward Bound to instil in our future managers the traits we can't foster in regular training – maturity, character, confidence, the will to succeed, and an addiction to excellence.'[17]

The (supposed) inherent values of sport have become accepted by many outside the Outward Bound movement and outside the sports themselves. Tutko and Bruns quote several prominent figures who have accepted these claims. General MacArthur stated: ['Sport] is a vital character builder. . . . It teaches [the youth of our country] to be proud and unbending in honest defeat, but humble and gentle in victory. . . . It gives them a predominance of courage over timidity, of appetite for adventure over loss of ease'. Similarly, Gerald Ford believes, 'there are few things more important to a country's growth and well-being than competitive athletics. If it is a cliché to say that athletics build character as well as muscle, then I subscribe to that cliché.'[18]

HABITS: SPORT AND MORAL TRAINING

I have taken a brief look at the background history that has influenced the formation of several beliefs relating the sporting environment to the enhancement of moral virtues. In particular, I have focused on the altruistic aspects of team sports (highlighted by the 'muscular Christian' gospel) and the friendship-forming qualities of climbing (stimulated by the 'kinship of the rope'). Both sets of situations are also believed to build character through challenge, struggle and perseverance.

At the start of this paper I mentioned that physical education provides many decision-provoking situations which allow 'practise' and, consequently, habitualisation of desirable behaviour. The sports highlighted in the historical background are ideal for presenting these situations. However, exposure alone does not guarantee a certain response. Whether these sports *do* develop moral qualities is a question that has been considered elsewhere.[19] Arguably, evidence suggesting that they *do not* is not proof that they *cannot*. Given that these situations arise, I shall first examine whether physical education *can* develop moral conduct.

Several important aspects arise from this preliminary discussion.

The first of these is the objective of habitualising desirable behaviour. Does sport serve the purpose of moral education if it provides such opportunities? Clearly, it does provide these situations. Durkheim suggest that these are part of an apprenticeship:

> There is a whole system of rules in the school that predetermine the child's conduct . . . a host of obligations that the child is required to shoulder. Together they constitute the discipline of the school. It is through the practise of school discipline that we can inculcate the spirit of discipline in the child.[20]

These obligations are 'act-orientated', concerning attendance at school, discipline in the classroom, doing homework, and so on. They are comparable with the act-orientated code of conduct that was upheld by the 'gentleman amateurs'. The discipline of the game situation *trains* a child for acceptance of the discipline of social conformity. This is the value of practising the 'acts' themselves.

The early stages of child development are pre-theoretical, in the sense that no reasons are given for why things should be so.[21] A child who asks why the ball is returned to the centre of the pitch after a goal is scored might be told that this is simply the way things are done. At this stage, the *principle* of fair play is not brought in. The child learns to perform acts as a integral part of a way of doing something. Most learning processes at this stage are situation specific. That is, we tell a child that such-and-such an act is 'naughty', but we do not attempt to explain how to prejudge which acts are 'naughty', and neither do we define what 'naughtiness' is. A further example of the act-orientation of the 'hidden curriculum' is the labelling of certain types of behaviour as good or bad. This is illustrated by the syllogism:

> Bad children are punished, and
> I was punished for kicking the goalkeeper.
> So, I must be a bad child

The deduction is invalid.[22] I have commited a punishable offence, which is not necessarily the act of a bad child. This helps to distinguish between what I have termed an 'act-orientation' and the utility of rules. The Victorian public school player held moral conduct to be identical in both sport and everyday life. Thus, if the act of cheating is 'bad', then anyone who cheats is behaving immorally. In contrast, the 'professional' tends to adopt a utilitarian outlook. The act in itself cannot be judged 'good' or 'bad' outside of the consequences. So it is not immoral to deliberately break a rule providing it is an open act that can be spotted by the referee and penalised.

Lawrence Kohlberg's theory of moral development consists of two 'preconventional' stages that correspond to what I have termed the 'pretheoretical' level.

> At this level the child is responsive to cultural rules and labels of good and bad, right or wrong, but interprets these labels in terms of either physical or hedonistic consequences of action (punishment, reward, exchange of favours) or in terms of the physical power of those who enunciate the rules and labels.[23]

The next stages after this are at the 'conventional' level. These stages are not prudentially orientated but concerned with maintaining and supporting the social order. This order is considered to be valuable in its own right. Stage three of development is the 'interpersonal concordance or "good boy–nice girl", orientation', and stage four is the 'law and order orientation'. The correct or right behaviour consists of adhering to stereotypical images, convention and authority.[24]

The four stages that make up Kohlberg's 'preconventional' and 'conventional' levels of moral development are concerned with the socialisation of individuals into desirable patterns of behaviour. This is covertly attempted in physical education by the habitual performance of moral actions, such as playing fairly, co-operating with team mates and showing restraint under pressure of defeat. It is not enough to *teach* what is right or wrong. It is for this reason that moral education is a latent function of the school. It is not taught directly as a subject, but indirectly through experience. Neumann suggests that children actually have to perform the actions themselves to internalise a desirable pattern of behaviour:

> The most important moral agency, when it is rightly inspired, is found in the actual performance of the pupils themselves. It is one thing to hear right conduct praised or to see it exemplified; it is quite another, and more necessary thing, for boys and girls themselves to do the acts. Character is essentially a matter of action, the habitual performance of certain kinds of deeds rather than others, and the only genuine way of learning how to do these deeds is to do them, just as the only way to learn tennis is to play.[25]

Is this notion of habit congruent with the meaning of moral behaviour?

Suppose we consider morality as the adoption of a social contract or universal ethical principles. Habitual behaviour need not necessarily be based on a grasp of any fundamental moral principles. Taking the ball to the centre circle to start the game might be the fairest way to begin, but is often done out of habit, without recognition of this (although the players might well recognise this, if they reflected on it). Consider an example where a golfer slices a shot into the trees. Having found the ball, the golfer takes several practice swings and then attempts a shot but only succeeds in burying the ball two inches deeper in the rough. This procedure is repeated again and again with the same results. Eventually, the golfer is successful and the players proceed up the fairway and complete the hole. On the next tee, the scorer asks the golfer for a total for the previous hole. The player hesitates and then adds up all the strokes in the trees and tells the scorer. Let us call this 'telling of the score' the *resultant action*. Suppose the player had hesitated because he or she thought that they could get away with declaring fewer strokes than they had played. Upon reflection, the golfer gave an honest assessment of the total. The 'resultant action' was the correct one. But was it morally good by virtue of its correctness? Let there be three alternatives to the golfer's reasoning behind the decision: (a) he or she would have cheated but was sure that one of the others had been counting the strokes; (b) his or her apprehension made them decide that honesty was the best policy; and (c) the golfer decided that cheating is wrong. In each case the 'resultant action' would be the same. However, if (a) was the case we would definitely not say that it was performed for moral reasons. We might also hesitate to say that (b) was performed for moral reasons. If 'honesty is the best policy' is a prudential principle that simply means 'dishonesty does not pay off in the long run', then (b) is not concerned with the morality of telling the truth, but rather its utility; (c) would be the only action based on moral reasoning. Thus, either the 'resultant action' is a moral one regardless of the reasons for its performance (which we would doubt in this example), or the performance must be accompanied by moral reasons. Arguably the latter is correct.

We could try to justify this further by showing that a child constrained to steal by a parent is not behaving immorally because he or she is forced to do it. In this case, the act cannot be separated from the circumstances of the producer. A court of law would have to judge the intent of the child. (A counter-argument here would be that the act itself is immoral, but that the child is absolved of any responsibility for its performance). However, would the child be acting immorally if he or she freely chose to steal (that is, without threat of punishment if he or she refused) but did so because of being socialised into stealing by the parents? Is this form of determined behaviour any different from the actions of the child brought up to be habitually 'good'? Kohlberg maintains that moral education should be concerned with principled moral judgements. This is reflected in our actions, but it is our judgements which are important. The inculcation of habits can be considered as more *training*. Kurt Baier distinguishes between this and moral *education:*

> The difference between moral training and moral education is that moral training is a process whereby a child acquires the morality of the community, whereas moral education is a deliberate activity, carried on primarily by professional teachers, for the purpose of fostering moral excellence in the young.[26]

Physical education faces two problems in the claim to be a moral educator. First if our code of conduct is act-orientated then these acts are legitimated pre-theoretically (without any attachment to their underlying principles), if they are inculcated as habits at an early age. Is this training or education? Secondly if we adopt a utilitarian approach to rules as simply constitutive components of a game, without moral content, then physical education teaches adherence to authority and not moral reasoning. Is this moral education or simply socialisation (even indoctrination)? These two problems might appear to disprove our claim that physical education can be a moral educator. However, it might be too presumptuous to associate habit (merely) with training.

THE PARADOX OF MORAL EDUCATION

This dilemma is not a new one. Its consideration has come to be termed 'the paradox of moral education'.[27] Kazepides summarises how the alleged paradox appears:

> When one thinks seriously about moral education one is struck by the apparent paradoxical nature of the whole enterprise, for it appears to be an attempt to develop (produce, engineer, create) the

rationally autonomous moral agent by non-rational means. Since we are often unable to communicate with young children in what we consider rational ways, we try to habituate them into desirable ways of behaving by some form of conditioning or we sometimes try to persuade them to act morally by offering them non-moral (e.g., prudential, utilitarian) reasons. Moreover, the relationship between the young and the adult moral authority is, at least initially, one of total dependence, a dependence deemed to be necessary as a condition for their gradual emancipation and development into autonomous moral agents.[28]

The origin of the paradox is the question of how virtue can be taught (raised by Socrates in discussion with Protagoras): is virtue the 'correct opinion' and conventional behaviour of well-brought-up people? Or is it conduct based on a group of fundamental moral principles? This clearly distinguishes 'virtue' as being associated either with the 'resultant action' or with the moral reasoning as discussed above. However, according to Peters, it was Aristotle who was led into the supposed paradox by his attempt to combine the two and stress the roles of both reason and habit.[29] Aristotle states, in the *Nichomachean Ethics:*

> One might be puzzled as to what we mean by saying that in order to become just, men must do just actions, and in order to become temperate they must do temperate actions. For if they do just and temperate actions, they are just and temperate already, just as if they spell correctly or play in tune, they are scholars and musicians.[30]

Taken out of context, Aristotle appears to be saying that in performing just actions we become just, but are already just by virtue of having performed these actions. So, a child is behaving morally even when behaving out of habit. However, Aristotle qualifies this by saying that the agents are behaving morally, only if (a) they know what they are doing; (b) they choose the act for its own sake; (c) they are consistent in these acts. In his words, 'the agent is just and temperate not when he does these acts merely, but when he does them *in the way* in which just and temperate men do them'.[31]

This leads me to comment on the second of the problems outlined earlier. The acceptance of the rules merely as a part of the game and not for their purpose of maintaining fair play is not an acceptance of the morality of sport. It is a utilitarian treatment of the rules as means to an end. This suggests that the sportworld is separate from the 'real world' and that our conduct in each is different. Sport serves little purpose as a 'training ground' if this is the case. Keating points out however,

> The source of the confusion which vitiates most discussion of sportsmanship is the unwarranted assumption that sport and athletics are so similar in nature that a single code of conduct and similar participant attitudes are applicable to both.

Let me make this distinction and limit my claims to 'sport' rather than including 'athletics' (the North American term for highly competitive and/or professional sport). Even accepting this, sport is limited as a tool of the moral educator. It cannot advance beyond Kohlberg's 'conventional level' of development, which emphasises adherence to authority and social norms.

The first of the two problems is still left to be discussed: are reason and habit compatible in moral education? It seems to be generally accepted that moral actions must be based on dispositions to act according to fundamental ethical principles. That is, the golfer is not acting morally by giving the correct score if this is not done with an acceptance of the 'rightness' of honesty. Peters tries to escape his own paradox by showing how it rests on a conceptual confusion about the meaning of 'habit'. That is, 'habit', as Peters proceeds to discuss it, does not necessarily exclude the use of intelligence. This is illustrated by the child's ability to separate an underlying rule or principle from the act itself. For instance, a parent who discovers their five-year-old daughter hitting her two-year-old brother over the head with a saucepan, and says 'Don't do that, it's naughty', does not mean 'Don't use a saucepan. It's naughty; you should use a hammer.' Moral *training* does not entail getting a child to perform faultlessly a fixed, habitual drill. Otherwise, the child would have to learn as many 'drills' as there might be situations to act upon. As Peters points out, 'the child has to learn to see that a vast range of very different actions and performances can fall under a highly abstract rule which makes them all examples of a type of action'.[33]

Habits without Reason: Etiquette and Indoctrination

The way to bring reason and habit together is to allow the learner the opportunity to make decisions for himself or herself in different situations. These decisions are based on principles that are abstracted from the acts themselves. Thus, we should teach what fair play means, rather than what constitutes an act of fair play. This is not always done. Even when teaching aspects of skill and strategy we do not always extract the principles from the instances. For example, the concept of 'good length' in squash is often taught using the example of the basic forehand or backhand 'drive'. As such, a 'good length' will be a shot that hits the front wall just above the cut line, bounces in, or around the area of, the service box and 'dies' in the back of the court. Students tend to focus on one or two aspects, such as getting the ball to bounce in the service box, and fail to recognise the underlying principle which allows for transference to other situations. Clearly, the service box has nothing to do with the concept of 'good length'. If the ball is hit very gently, it will need to be hit higher up the front wall and land further back down the court in order 'to die' in the back corner. The inability to see the commonalities in different actions undoubtedly exists in everyday occurrences.

Contradictions are particularly apparent between similar acts in sport (as well as between attitudes and behaviour). Players ceremoniously shake hands before an important soccer game and exchange shirts afterwards (usually quite amicably and sincerely). Yet, throughout the game they verbally harass, spit at, punch and trip their immediate opponents. These are contradictions that occur when the etiquette of the sport has been habitualised. However, the habitualisation of sporting etiquette is *not* moral education. There is little or no carry-over from the situation-specific mores of particular sports like cricket and golf to more general instances.

Given that moral education requires the teaching of reasoned principles, I need to draw a further distinction between the uses of socialisation and indoctrination. Indoctrination is a very emotive term and few parents or educators would admit that they in any way indoctrinate. Let me determine exactly what is meant by the term. Indoctrination is quite distinct from conditioning or from the use of force. Suppose we bring up our children to be repulsed at the thought of masturbating. A child might understand that there is nothing wrong with masturbating, but nevertheless feels strongly against doing it himself. This is 'conditioning'. If a parent tries to prevent the child from masturbating by threat of punishment, then this is 'force' or 'constraint'. However, indoctrination occurs when the child is persuaded not to masturbate by being given reasons that are either false or indefensible. For instance, the parents might say, 'If you masturbate, you won't be able to have children.' Surprisingly, we indoctrinate a great deal of time when we try to socialise children into a certain behaviour which we cannot justify. Many parents use an 'appeal to a higher authority' because they do not know how to determine why things are right or wrong, or what reasons they can give the child. So, a child is taught not to do certain things because God will punish them, or because Father Christmas does not bring toys to naughty children. Nearly all teaching of etiquette and manners is, in some way, a form of indoctrination, unless taught so as to make it clear that they are simply social customs.

The resort to accepting behaviour as social customs is, in fact, a less obvious form of indoctrination. Indoctrination applies to any method which consciously attempts to implant a dogmatic belief that is causally motivated, rather than rationally motivated. Consequently, the believer might be able to give reasons for the belief, but these will not be the true motivators of this – they will simply be rationalisations. That is, in this instance, the reasons themselves are not causally operative in the belief. The dogmatic obedience to authority or custom is often mistaken for morality. Thus, in physical education, it is not enough to teach people the etiquette of the game, or to teach players to obey the rules on the basis of the acceptance of the authority of the referee. If sport is used, in this respect, to train children to accept the legal system, then it is not moral education.

Habits Based on Principles

Undoubtedly, a child cannot always grasp a principle, and rarely comprehends the reasons behind the principle. The training of habits must take place during these formative years. However, the onus is on the educator to be able to justify the habits which are being formed. One result of this is that moral education cannot remain a 'hidden' part of the curriculum, to be undertaken haphazardly by teachers unaware of their role in these formative years. The physical educator must be aware himself or herself of the moral principles affecting our conduct in sport.

As the child becomes more able to reason, the emphasis of moral education changes to accommodate the different stages of moral development. Kohlberg's last stage is the 'universal ethical-principle orientation'.

Right is defined by the decision on conscience in accord with self-chosen *ethical principles* appealing to logical comprehensiveness, universality, and consistency. These principles are abstract and ethical (the Golden Rule, the categorical imperative): they are universal principles of justice, of the reciprocity and equality of human rights and of respect for the dignity of human beings as individual persons.[34]

The consequences of this approach to moral education can be summarised with respect to the claims that sport is a 'training ground'. As I have shown, the Victorian code of 'gentlemanly conduct' is based on the acceptance of acts, normally associated with the very specific etiquette of a particular game. Golf is one sport with an abundance of conventional procedures such as this. There are often (good) reasons behind the formation of these manners, but they are rarely mentioned in the habitualisation of newcomers into the customs. While these acts remain separated from any underlying principles they are of little or no use to educators. The character-building claims of these sports are more vague and harder to pin down. But clearly, the numerous incidents involving false claims of first ascents in the mountains give strong evidence that climbing itself has little effect on character. It is certainly not as Douglas would have us believe: 'I have never met along the trails of the high mountains a mean man, a man who would cheat or steal.'[35] This leads me to the 'kinship of the rope'. Klaus Meier has assessed this claim and argued that such friendship, if founded on the 'loving struggle', are 'existentially deficient'. He notes that:

If the nature and comprehensiveness of the relationship between individuals are based solely upon the immediate concreteness of the situation and are limited to specifiable, utilitarian or pragmatic intentions or purposes (such as solving a particular problem posed by the configuration of a section of the mountain), the communication manifested, in a very different sense, may be termed impersonal. . . . The perceived significance of this type of camaraderie is based upon task fulfillment rather than full and authentic interpersonal communication.[36]

Finally, if habits and reasons can be in some way combined, whereby one assumes principles as a matter of habit until able to reason their justification (or change one's principles), then sport does have a role to play as part of moral education. Peters suggests that we are able to 'enter the Palace of Reason through the Courtyard of Habit and Tradition'.[37] This we are able to do if our learning of games is based on an understanding of what it is to play a game. Moral education can become a part of physical education if the playing of sport is informed by a comprehension and reasoning of the purposes of constitutive rules and the maintenance of fair play. If this becomes the case, not only will sport provide situations where our conduct has a bearing on all aspects of our life, but moreover, the two situations will be based on the same dispositions and actions. Morality in sport and morality in all other spheres are inextricably intertwined. As Hirst says:

> For the fully consistent moral life, the dispositions must also be in keeping with the same rules and principles. It would in fact seem to be the case that what we usually mean by a virtue or a vice (say honesty or cruelty) is not simply the disposition to think and act so spontaneously and even unconsciously. The dispositions of the moral life therefore need to be all of a piece and consistently related to the person's underlying moral rules and principles.[38]

Notes

1. It is worth mentioning John Rawls' highly acclaimed and much discussed *A Theory of Justice* (Cambridge, Mass., 1971) which is in part based on exactly this correspondence. Rawls' initial outline for his thesis was presented in his 1958 paper 'Justice as Fairness'.
2. Notice how the relationship between sport and society is one-way in all our examples. That is, sport is subordinate to, or less valuable than, 'everyday life' (whatever this might be). Consequently, sport and physical education can be justified to some extent by playing a part in more 'serious' aspects of life, which are (presumably) inherently justifiable. In this view the 'sportsworld' is always the training ground for the 'real world', and vice versa.
3. P. J. Arnold, *Education, Physical Education and Personality Development* (New York, 1968) p. 104.
4. See E. D. Mitchell and B. S. Mason, *The Theory of Play* (New York, 1948) pp. 288–9. Cf. Arnold, *Education, Physical Education and Personality Development*, pp. 107–8.
5. Arnold, ibid., p. 107.
6. G. Redmond, 'The First Tom Brown's Schooldays: Origins and Evolution of "Muscular Christianity" in Children's Literature, 1762–1857', *Quest* vol. xxx, (Summer 1978) p. 7. Redmond also points out that 'to play fairly and avoid cheating were sentiments which were reiterated time and again in the *sports* books produced for children in the first-half of the nineteenth century' (p. 14).

7. See P. C. McIntosh, *Sport in Society* (London, 1979) p. 77.
8. See P. C. McIntosh, *Fair Play: Ethics in Sport and Education* (London, 1979) p. 33.
9. E. Newby, *Great Ascents: A Narrative History of Mountaineering* (London, 1977) p. 41.
10. Professor John Tyndall was a contemporary of Faraday and succeeded him at the Royal Institute. He was one of the last of the scientist mountaineers who was first attracted to the mountains to collect evidence for a theory of glaciation, but became fascinated by the sport.
11. Cf. Newby, *Great Ascents,* p. 41.
12. A. Hankinson, *The Mountain Men: An Early History of Rock Climbing in North Wales* (London, 1977) p. 1.
13. William Wordsworth, *Lines Composed a Few Miles above Tintern Abbey* (cf. Hankinson, *The Mountain Men* p. 2).
14. P. Donnelly, 'The Last of Four Fallacies: Climbing Leads People to Form Close Friendship', *Mountain,* vol. 83 (Jan./Feb. 1982) p. 45.
15. C. S. Houston, 'The Last Blue Mountain', in S.Z. Klausner (ed.), *Why Man Takes Chances: Studies in Stress Seeking* (New York, 1968) p. 51. Cf. Donnelly 'The Last of Four Fallacies' p. 45.
16. A. D. Munrow, *Physical Education: A Discussion of Principles* (London, 1972), p. 143.
17. Cf. Donnelly 'The Third of Four Fallacies: Climbing is Character Building', *Mountain,* vol. 82 (Nov./Dec. 1981) p. 20.
18. T. Tutko and W. Bruns, 'Sports Don't Build Character – They Build Characters', in D. Stanley Eitzen, *Sport in Contemporary Society: An Anthology* (New York, 1979) pp. 234–5.
19. P. C. Donnelly, 'The Four Fallacies', *Mountain,* nos. 80–3 (1981–2).
20. E. Durkheim, *Moral Education* (Glencoe, Ill., 1961) p. 148.
21. P. L. Berger and T. Luckmann, *The Social Construction of Reality* (New York, 1966) pp. 94–5.
22. The minor premise 'affirms the consequent' which does not entail that the subject of this premise belongs to the class of things described in the antecedent of the major premise. This might be clearer in the following example: All rabbits eat carrots. I eat carrots. Therefore, I am a rabbit. Obviously, it is not only rabbits that eat carrots, so associating myself with carrot-eaters does not mean that I am a rabbit.
23. L. Kohlberg, 'Stages of Moral Development as a Basis for a Moral Education', in C. M. Beck, B. S. Crittenden, and E. V. Sullivan (eds), *Moral Education: Interdisciplinary Approaches* (Toronto, 1971) p. 86.
24. Ibid., p. 87.
25. H. Neumann, *Education for Moral Growth* (New York, 1923) p. 191.
26. K. Baier, 'Ethical Pluralism and Moral Education', in Beck *et al., Moral Education,* p. 95.
27. R. S. Peters, 'Reason and Habit: The Paradox of Moral Education', in W. R. Niblett (ed.), *Moral Education in a Changing Society* (London, 1963) pp. 46–65.
28. T. Kazepides, 'The Alleged Paradox of Moral Education', in D. B. Cochrane, C. H. Hamm and A. C. Kazepides, *The Domain of Moral Education* (New York, 1979) p. 155.

29. Peters, 'Reason and Habit', p. 47.
30. Aristotle, *Nicomachean Ethics*, ıı. iv. 1.
31. Ibid., ıı.iv. 4–5.
32. J. W. Keating, 'Sportsmanship as a Moral Category' *Ethics*, vol. 74 (Oct. 1964) p. 34, reprinted in E. W. Gerber and W. J. Morgan, *Sport and the Body*, pp. 264–71.
33. Peters, 'Reason and Habit', p. 62.
34. Kohlberg, 'Stages of Moral Development as a Basis for Moral Education', p. 88.
35. W. O. Douglas quoted in G. A. Smith and C. D. Smith (eds), *The Armchair Mountaineer* (New York, 1968) p. 23.
36. K. Meier, 'The Kinship of the Rope and the Loving Struggle: A Philosophic Analysis of Communication in Mountain Climbing', *Journal of the Philosophy of Sport*, vol. 3, (1979) pp. 57–8.
37. Peters, 'Reason and Habit', p. 55.
38. P. Hirst, *Moral Education in a Secular Society* (London, 1974) p. 67.

8

Playing the Game: Morality versus Leisure

TOM WINNIFRITH

There's a breathless hush in the Close tonight–
    Ten to make and the match to win –
A bumping pitch and a blinding light,
    An hour to play and the last man in
And it's not for the sake of a ribboned coat,
    Or the selfish hope of a season's fame,
But his Captain's hand on his shoulder smote –
    'Play up! play up! and play the game!'

The sand of the desert is sodden red –
    Red with the wreck of a square that broke; –
The Gatling's jammed and the Colonel dead,
    And the regiment blind with dust and smoke.
The river of death has brimmed his banks,
    And England's far, and Honour a name,
But the voice of a schoolboy rallies the ranks
    'Play Up! play up! and play the game!'[1]

What game? The game in the first stanza of Henry Newbolt's poem 'Vitai Lampada' is, of course, cricket, although not the kind of cricket first-class cricketers play now when there are light meters to prevent the light from being too blinding and helmets to prevent the pitch from bumping the batsman too hard. The second game is war, presumably, since there is a reference to the desert and Newbolt was writing before the First World War, one of those messy colonial wars of which we are now ashamed. It is easy to pour scorn on Newbolt, a man who wrote a poem in which he called Clifton the best of schools and sent his son to Winchester. His praise of patriotism, of imperialism, of foreign wars and heroes of the Empire seems as outdated as his philosophy on

149

games as part of his grand scheme is confused. In a curious way, however, in an age where games have become like warfare and warfare has lost any vestiges of chivalry we occasionally find ourselves pining nostalgically for the confident if muddled views of Newbolt, although in considering games as part of leisure we are clearly in difficulties if we follow Newbolt and see games as means to a sterner moral end.

Newbolt's views may seem at first sight period pieces, but they did survive the battle of the Somme and the introduction of bodyline until the time of my youth in the decade after the Second World War when my mentors, gnarled old Anglo-Indian warriors and cricket blues, taught me the importance of cricket, of fair play, of playing with a straight bat, of games as a preparation for the battle of life, of games as moulding character and inevitably of England as the place where these virtues flourished best, therefore making England greater than any other nation. The triumphs of the West Indies in cricket and the Argentinians and Brazilians at football were still to come, as were the terrible scenes of hooliganism which have resulted in spectators from the United Kingdom, inventor of so many games, being banned from attending football matches in Europe.

Even before these disasters there were still gaping holes in the argument of Newbolt and the schoolmasters of my youth. Playing the game has come to mean the same as fair play of sportsmanship. It is not clear just how Newbolt's heroes display this latter virtue. In the first stanza the last man in will have to display courage and skill in defending his wicket against hostile bowling on a bumping pitch and in a blinding light, and his captain is exhorting him to display these virtues in order that the ten runs may be scored and the match won. But he is not exactly urging fair play on him. Likewise the young subaltern who rallies the ranks is hardly appealing to them to make the fight more fair by, for instance, encouraging them to hand their Gatling, jammed or not, to the attacking tribesmen. It might be useful to distinguish between playing up, playing to win and playing the game, behaving in a sportsmanlike manner. Playing up has unfortunate connotations in the teaching profession who do not like to see their students so behaving. Perhaps this is why my teachers avoided the phrase. Even without this extra source of confusion they seemed peculiarly keen that the side in which I was playing should be victorious, and when it lost, as it usually did, used, in a way that I found hard to understand, to accuse us of bad sportsmanship. Had my school been one in which the pupils played up their masters I would have dared to raise the objection that we were playing for our enjoyment and amusement, or even quoted Newbolt and said I 'loved the game beyond the prize'.[2] I would then have been accused of being incurably frivolous; had my teachers known the right modern phrase they would have said 'don't play games with me'.

We do now seem to have our first source of confusion in an area where playing language games is not going to help us. Clearly, playing to win involves a different sort of attitude from playing fair. To take some obvious examples – walking at cricket when the umpire gives you out, or even before; helping an injured opponent off the ground at football; giving away a point at tennis after a dubious line call in your favour – clearly do not help you to win the game, but are signs of a good sportsman. Rolling on the ground in order to attract the referee's attention; running out the batsman at the bowler's end, and coughing when your opponent is about to putt for the match, are designed to win the match, but such tactics are frowned upon. When in a celebrated incident the Australian captain ordered one of his bowlers to deliver the last ball of the match along the ground in order to prevent the opposing batsman hitting a six to win, he was playing up, although paradoxically bowling down, but he was emphatically not playing the game.

In an effort to keep both playing up and playing the game in the same category we have to rely heavily on team games, where certain activities like hogging the bowling while not scoring fast, or trying to score a try on your own with two men outside you are clearly examples of putting the desire for individual glory above team success, while certain other actions like selflessly sacrificing your wicket or the opportunity to score a goal in order that the side may win are clearly both playing up and playing the game. Hence the greater credit given to games like cricket and football as opposed to individual sports like golf or tennis or even running, in spite of the fact that the latter are more enjoyable ways of spending leisure hours. They involve less danger, effort and periods of boredom, there are more opportunities to meet and compete with members of the opposite sex, and these games can be played at a much greater age.

Cricket and football offer other opportunities both for playing up and playing the game. Success in both sports depends upon a strange mixture of strength, skill, speed, endurance and luck which are not present in, for example, chess or snooker, and such success is hedged about by complicated rules and strategies which are not really present in golf or lawn tennis or running. It is fairly difficult to cheat at golf and tennis and, *pace* Stephen Potter, gamesmanship in these two games has only a limited number of ploys which can be used.[3] At cricket and association football, apart from the examples already mentioned, there are many ways of appealing to the referee, wasting time and intimidating the opposition, while rugby football is a game so complicated that it is almost impossible not to break the rules, especially in the scrum, about once a minute. All these games present a delicate balance between gamesmanship and fair play which must make them the despair of philosophers and referees alike. Possibly it is the finding of this delicate balance that is playing the game. In this case, after initially finding that there was an equation between fair play and playing the game we now seem to be saying that playing the game is not more than a penalty spot on the fair field of fair play. This would seem to confirm the view that professional gamesplayers who take on the arduous task of finding this spot are not really enjoying leisure at all.

Let us leave this confusion and turn to another, implicit in Newbolt's poem where the game of cricket is linked to the fame of war. But war is not a game, as Huizinga clearly saw when he wrote *Homo Ludens*.⁴ Huizinga, writing before Hitler handled the ball of war and before the institution of most of the horrors of modern professional sport, is a perceptive if pessimistic analyst of man's decline in both war and sport and the strange way in which men have tried to link the two. It is true that more distinguished poets than Newbolt have tried to connect war and sport. Virgil borrowed the idea of funeral games from Homer and made some fairly obvious references to playing the game, since those heroes who do not bend the rules and those who are virtuous win both in games and in battle.⁵ It is equally true that some aspects of warfare as for example siegecraft in the Middle Ages, have the air of an elaborate game, whereby slowly over the centuries people learned to cope with bumping cannon balls by introducing helmets for their walls. Huizinga has some interesting things to say about medieval jousts. But philosophers rather than students of literature and history will protest that war cannot be a game, since, though it has an essential feature of a game – the need to win – there are rules in games to ensure that winning is fair, while in war this is not so.

That games require winning is, I think, a truism. We have special names for activities like games which do not require winning, such as kickabout, knockup, net, sparring match, trial run. Even in solitary games like patience we have to beat a system if the patience is to come out. In trying to distinguish games from other forms of leisure Socrates and some others might well put philosophy into the category of games, leisure activities which involve competition which in turn involves victory and defeat. So perhaps the schoolmasters of my youth were right in stressing the importance of winning. The game is worth more than the prize, but without any prize there is no game. With war the prize is clearly more important than the game, but not only is war, like professional sport, clearly not a leisure activity, but also it does not have any rules.

Various attempts have been made to impose rules and referees on warfare. The Geneva Convention, the League of Nations, successive peace treaties and even the court of public opinion have been appealed to, but not very often by Hitler or very successfully by the victims of Hiroshima. War games, a misleading name for practice manoeuvres, have umpires and rules but they are not in the same relationship to war as knockabouts are to football. Games have partisan spectators, but these are not, or should not be, involved in the action (although regrettably in the last twenty years they have become so) just as two hundred years ago civilians were not really involved in wars. Milton in describing the War in Heaven declared that in comparison with it all other war seemed a civil game,[6] and previous wars may seem this to our generation.

Nevertheless, wars and games are distinct. Why then did Newbolt and a whole range of Englishmen from the middle of the nineteenth century to the middle of the twentieth persist in thinking that a training in sport was an admirable preparation not only for war, but for a whole host of other activities as well? Only the British thought this, and with a few exceptions it is only in Britain and her former colonies that we find the typically English team games of rugby and cricket played, games with most complicated rules and interesting moral undertones. A variety of reasons can be found for this peculiar insular trait; our job is to work out whether it is right or wrong to say that a man who plays with a straight bat in cricket will play with a straight bat in life. As students of leisure we must note that once games have acquired this aura of moral education they cease to be leisure pursuits.

There are however empirical ways of casting doubt on the assertion that success in sporting activity leads to success in other spheres. Recent examples of sportsmen like Best and Higgins, ruined before the age of thirty-five, are perhaps unfair as they have been spoilt not by too much sport or too little leisure, but by early wealth and the attention of the media. It is easier to name earlier cricketers who died by their own hand or of drink, or earlier footballers who died as paupers. It is difficult to prove that those who succeed in life after being successful in sport derive their success in one from their success in the other. Lord Rothschild and Samuel Beckett are an improbable pair of first-class cricketers, unlikely to claim that their high reputation in other spheres owed much to cricket. Certain professions, such as public school headmasters, do seem to attract more than their fair share of games players, but no doubt this can be attributed to the vested interests of a charmed closed circle. There seems no particular logical reason why skill at batting or bowling or kicking or passing should qualify one to be a good judge or general or stockbroker or headmaster. It could be argued that success in one sphere might be a harbinger of success in another endeavour, but we do not seem to apply the same principle to successful stamp collectors or bell ringers or trombone players, all practitioners of perfectly harmless leisure activities, but seen in a different light from cricketers and football players.

In the bad old days of the British Empire people used to say that the Sudan was a place where blacks were governed by blues. The idea that games, particularly team games involving contests, and more particularly the games of cricket, rugby and soccer, prepared one to administer justice may seem an odd one. It is not just a matter of understanding and laying down complicated rules. Curiously enough, bellringing involves complicated rules and contests, and is a team sport, but nobody ever said Bechuanaland was run by bellringers. Nor, more importantly, does it seem that games are all concerned with justice. An important concept in jurisprudence is the *mens rea*. Football tries to do its best to distinguish intentional and unintentional breakers of its laws with such terms as accidental offside and professional foul. But this is a hard task, and we have seen earlier that one way of playing the game successfully is taking risks and steering just the right side of the law. This kind of games playing would seem to be a better qualification for being a stockbroker than for being a colonial administrator or a judge, three professions which have all beeen successfully filled by sportsmen. Sentences like 'he bamboozled the batsman with his googly' or 'he deceived the fullback with his dummy' or 'he lured the striker into the offside trap' all give the impression that sportsmen are better poachers than gamekeepers. Sensible views of justice as fair play, preached eloquently by Rawls,[7] appear to fall foul of the fact that fair play is not really very fair.

Huizinga, usually keen on etymology, misses a trick when in his discussion of play and the law he fails to note that the Greek word *agon*, a contest, is used both to describe athletic bouts and cases in the law courts. Huizinga is full of subtle reminders of the ways in which legal cases resemble sporting occasions, though the cricket analogy perhaps escaped him. In legal cases, as in cricket, defending and prosecuting council take alternate innings as in cricket, occasionally appealing to the judge as umpire, whom they treat with great respect, but regard with great hostility if he is opposed to them. Like the law, games have a set of rules which subtly change as various precedents are set, and as in the law these rules are meant to be fair, though sometimes they seem a bit of an ass. Cricketers become umpires in the same way that advocates become judges, and oddly enough the best advocates and cricketers are not always the best judges and umpires. But as with war, so it is with law. In the law the rules are the game, whereas in games the rules are a tiresome obtrusion. The best lawyers know the rules best, but this is clearly not the case with games.

The Newboltian thesis is that games, particularly our famous and stern games which I shall call agonistic games, are good things in themselves, the sterner and the more agonistic the better and that part or all of their goodness lies in the preparation for the great game of life.

There is a slightly more modern version of Newbolt, written by Sir Frederick Toone, manager of the England cricket team to Australia on three occasions in the 1920s. He is talking of cricket before the bodyline controversy, but even so there is a quaint if moving air about what he says:

> It [cricket] is a science, the study of a lifetime, in which you may exhaust yourself, but never your subject. It is a contest, a duel or mêlée calling for courage, skill, strategy and self-control. It is a contest of temper, a trial of honour, a revealer of character. It affords a chance to play the man and act the gentleman. It means going into God's out of doors, getting close to nature, fresh air exercise, a sweeping away of mental cobwebs, genuine recreation of the tired tissues. It is a cure for care, an antidote for worry. It includes companionship with friends, social intercourse, opportunities for courtesy, kindliness and generosity to an opponent. It promotes not only physical health, but mental force.[8]

Jardine and Larwood, though strong on physical health and mental force, were not great ones for promoting courtesy, kindliness or generosity, and were hardly antidotes to worry for the next harassed manager. And yet although in practice the aims of cricketers and other sportsmen at the highest level have been sadly tarnished, most professionals being clearly motivated by a desire for success, fame and material rewards, we still retain something of Toone's idealism. Rawls certainly sees games as having different sorts of ends, not just the desire to win. He says that players may have different motives for playing, mentioning exercise and excitement among them, then declares that there is a social purpose, not perhaps observed by the players, and finally mentions 'the shared end, the common desire of all the players that there should be a good play of the game'.[9]

Occasionally in professional sport we find players joining with partisan spectators in rejoicing that the game is a good one even though their side has lost. Though a good play of the game is not a phrase that has entered the English language in quite the same way as playing up or playing the game, it does as an end in itself seem to get round the objection we have found in a number of attitudes to games as part of leisure. If games are intended to make the player richer, stronger, more famous or even more virtuous, then they are not pure forms of leisure. It is true that a great many games do have these benefits, nor should we sneer at all of them as goals for the games player. Though the benefits to health and strength of playing games can be exaggerated, as many an arthritic jogger or injured footballer has found, doctors do prescribe exercise as a benefit. The moral improvement on which we have cast some doubts is clearly less tangible, but sloth, selfishness, silliness and superbia, pride, the root of all sins, are vices which games are supposed to eradicate, and there is a good deal to suggest that they do.

Games involve practice before the contest and effort during it. Nothing is worse for a gamesplayer than feeling he or she has not given his or her best during game. Almost as bad is the feeling of being out of practice or training. There is not much room in football or cricket for a lazy or selfish player. Prima donna behaviour may be fostered by the media, but the stern game soon finds out and then turns on gifted artists like McEnroe. Eccentric behaviour is frowned upon in sport, although odd little quirks like Jardine's Harlequin cap have a certain charm. There is no point in being silly in sport; the fly kick, the Chinese cut, the cunning back pass are cruelly punished. Modesty in success, not boasting about one's achievements, not crowing over one's enemy's discomfiture, not blaming others for one's failings, not questioning the rules, learning to be a good loser, are precious virtues that games can and should teach us, although both on the sports field and in life wingeing and whining, boasting and lying are becoming all too prevalent.

But sport as a moral educator, valuable though it may be, seems to take it out of the category of a leisure activity. Professional cricketers who take time off from cricket to play golf or visit nightclubs are publicly reprimanded, though perhaps secretly admired, but we have already seen reasons for removing professional sport from the sphere of leisure. Games, especially agonistic games, that are played to improve the character, would also seem too stern to be counted as part of leisure. In spite of the associations of *scholē* with leisure, sport as a part of education seems to lack that element of enjoyment, if not of frivolity, which seems to be one of the elements of leisure. We may note in passing that the words 'sport' and 'sportsman' have a slightly loftier and more moral tone than games and gamesplayer. I am a sportsman, you are a gamesplayer, he wastes his time in trivial pursuits.

And yet it will be argued, in spite of Newbolt on the one hand and the iniquities of professional sportsmen on the other, that sport and games of one kind or another represent a main strand, if not the main strand, of leisure. Here we return to Rawls and note his clumsily expressed but essentially right final goal for people playing games, that there should be a good play of the game. This goodness is not moral, but aesthetic. A good game is not one which produces heroes or judges or statesmen, but one which intrigues, excites and satisfies. Hardbitten journalists employ clichés about artists and craftsmen on the sportsfield, but these clichés like the well worn dramatic imagery used to describe exciting matches, do spring from the feeling that a good game, like a great work of art and a great play, is good in itself. Pictures and plays can be enjoyed, though in a different way, by both artists and performers on the one hand, and spectators on the other.

Many games are, of course, bad works of art. The vagaries of the weather wash out some completely. In others, the contestants are so ill-matched that the result becomes wholly predictable. We would not think much of a play that peters out in the second act, or one in which the conclusion is glaringly obvious at about the same time, and yet many games are played in precisely this way. Others are not. It is one of the charms of our great agonistic games that the unexpected *peripeteia* can take place. When in a celebrated cricket match England beat Australia after being forced to follow on, the Australian captain, who in a subsequent match lost Newboltian admirers through bursting into tears, won many hearts by declaring that the result was good for cricket. Captains, of course, especially in cricket, can do a great deal to ensure exciting and interesting finishes, very often having to cast aside thoughts of winning in the process. Playing up does not always ensure a good play of the game.

So much for the game as a whole. Individual players can still give pleasure to themselves, the spectators and even their opponents by an artistic stroke, a fine run or a good save, and these individual exploits can enliven the dying embers of a dull game that is already lost or won. Such exploits must of course take place within the rules of the game. A no ball cannot be a good ball. On the other hand, individual feats of excellence do not have much to do with fair play. In a way it seems unfair that some players can effortlessly stroke the ball to the boundary or swerve past approaching tacklers, while all that honest effort can do is to stop the ball or be in a position to tackle. Genius in sport does not seem to be an infinite capacity for taking pains; if it were, we might take a leisure activity too seriously.

In a useful if slightly irritating series of essays on games,[10] Suits does draw attention to the many paradoxes inherent in games. We have shown that it is often difficult both to play up and play the game, since playing ruthlessly to win would seem sometimes to demand a cynical manipulation or disregard of the rules of the game. Simultaneously playing up often ensures that there is not a good play of the game, since little aesthetic enjoyment is derived from a victory that is a walkover. Plays in which all suspense is over in the first act and monochrome paintings hardly excite or inspire. And yet without the desire to win, which is an element of playing up, games are hardly games.

Games are also suspect as forms of leisure if they are regarded as moral training, valuable though that training may be, and odd though it is that we tend to see more moral training in the games which are famous for playing up, playing the game and in which there may be a good play of the game. Nobody ever said that playing shove-halfpenny made a better person, and shove-halfpenny is rather a boring game; but games which are treated as a kind of religion have ceased to be games. The moral training of games is surely to be seen in the way that the player of them has to balance the different goals of the game. Life is perhaps less simple with its paradoxes less clear cut, but in it too we find a variety of ends, in the achieving of which we have to sacrifice other prizes. In his baffled way Newbolt was probably right in seeing some kind of connection between the cricket field and the bloodsodden desert, though wrong in thinking that the only object of the schoolboy was or should have been to score the ten runs or rally his ranks.

Notes

1. H. Newbolt, *Collected Poems, 1897–1907* (London, 1907) pp. 131–2.
2. H. Newbolt, 'Clifton Chapel', in *Collected Poems*, p. 128.

3. S. Potter's observations in *The Theory and Practice of Gamesmanship: or the Art of Winning Games Without Actually Cheating* (London, 1947) have become so universally accepted that the word *gamesmanship,* meaning manipulation of the rules of the game to one's own advantage, and *ploy,* designating a manoeuvre towards this end, have entered the English language. Potter was not, of course, being wholly serious, and was writing in an age when sportsmanship rather than gamesmanship was more in evidence. Fortunately nobody talks of 'ploying the game'.

4. J. Huizinga, *Homo Ludens: A Study of the Play Element in Culture* (London, 1949). Though not translated into English until 1949, Huizinga wrote his book in Dutch in 1938.

5. Virgil *Aeneid,* Book v. Nisus does bend the rules when after a collision with Salius, reminiscent of Mary Decker and Zola Budd, he allows Euryalus to come through and win. Later, in Book ix, he and Euryalus both suffer through being too eager to win glory. Piety wins first place for Cloanthus and Acestes in Book v; Dares and Sergestes are not sportsmen, and lose.

6. John Milton, *Paradise Lost,* vi. 667.

7. J. Rawls, *A Theory of Justice* (Oxford, 1972).

8. To be found in B. Green (ed.), *Wisden Anthology, 1900–1940* (London, 1980) p. 918.

9. Rawls, *A Theory of Justice,* p. 525.

10. R. Suits, *The Grasshopper: Games, Life and Utopia* (Toronto, 1978).

9

French Intellectuals and Leisure: the Case of Emmanuel Mounier

BRIAN RIGBY

There is a specifically French tradition of writing on leisure which one can trace at least from the 1930s to the middle of the 1960s.[1] This tradition certainly had important historical antecedents and it would be more than rash to claim that it had played itself out by the 1960s, but this period of over thirty years seems on balance to mark the heyday of a particular French approach to thinking about leisure. In this short study I do not intend to describe the overall nature of this tradition but rather to focus on what I consider to be one central aspect; namely, the key role played by the progressive Catholic philosopher of personalism, Emmanuel Mounier. Personalism seems never really to have attracted a great interest, and this is no doubt to a significant degree due to the fact that in the early postwar period it was overshadowed by the more spectacular success of Sartrean existentialism, with which personalism had some close affinities. In fact, although existentialism had a great appeal for sections of the general public, as well as, of course, for academics and intellectuals, it is by no means going too far to suggest that personalism had a far more important influence in shaping public debates on 'cultural' matters.[2] Not least, personalism remained for many years an inspiration for those postwar cultural 'animateurs' who were responsible for putting into practice programmes and policies of leisure:[3]

His [Mounier's] work did not result in a plan, a programme, organisational structures, but it inspired and still inspires – particularly in the field of art and cultural action – a large number of those people who chose this area of activity for their social commitment. His work encourages people not to be content with the economic or the social dimension of life, but to give full weight to politics, while at the same time, for example, respecting the person's creative capacity, whereas consumer society only seems to recognise in man a producer (in his work) or a consumer (in his leisure).[4]

My main interest here, however, is not to study those cultural 'animateurs' and thinkers influenced by Mounier, but rather to go back and look closely at the writings of Mounier himself and, in particular, to set out his reflections upon leisure.

An article written by François Henry in 1937 on 'Leisure and the Human Person' can serve as a useful introduction to the subject of personalism and leisure.[5] The crucial passage of Henry's article is the following:

Without it being in any way a question of disdaining the place of rest, entertainment or necessary relaxation, we will remind you that our principal aim is not to make leisure activities exclusively into forms of *diversion* [*divertissements*], in the deepest sense of the word, that is to say activities which turn us away from life, while occupying us with simply anything in order to kill time and dispel boredom; our ideal is to see in leisure a form of *culture* which will develop a life rooted in the real. Culture is the opposite of diversion, for instead of turning its back on what exists, it in fact respects it and highlights it. If we can maintain this meaning in leisure, then everyone in his free time will be able to rediscover the unity of his life beyond the daily dispersal of the self: a unity which will enable the human person to blossom. It is this unity of leisure and work which is expressed in these words: God gave a garden to Adam so that in cultivating it he might cultivate himself.[6]

As this passage indicates, the aim of personalism was to encourage the full blossoming of 'the person' by achieving a unity in the self, a unity made up both of social action and spiritual development. A Pascalian notion of *divertissement* leads to a rejection of that kind of leisure in which one is deflected from the truly important things of life, and in which one seeks escape from boredom in gratuitous and trivial activity. Finding the word 'leisure' to be tainted with connotations of distraction and entertainment, Henry prefers the word 'culture', which evidently provides the desired connotations of education and self-development. The interesting expression 'daily dispersal of the self' indicates that Henry believes that leisure time, far from being the occasion for loss and 'dispersal' of the self, should in fact be the time for reassembling the fragments into an orderly, unified whole. Many of these themes in Henry's article recur in Mounier's work, where we also find a similar desire to reject distraction in favour of spiritual 'concentration'.

In this article Henry also focused on another aspect of leisure which was at the centre of Mounier's preoccupations, and which was closely linked with the political issues of the day. While recognising that the 'organisation' of leisure was inevitable in modern society, Henry expressed the fear that this organisation might follow the fascist or totalitarian models. Henry's fear was that initiatives, such as those to be found in contemporary Germany, where, for example, workers went on collective holidays in order to share a communal, 'democratic' style of living, did not in fact tend to support the personalist aims of self-development and growth in moral awareness, but rather tended to subordinate the individual to an anonymous mass, and to lead to a loss of personal freedom.[7] The great dilemma of the day, according to Henry, was how to deal with 'the inhuman and absolute primacy of the group'.[8] At a time when leisure was being used more and more by governments as a political tool for controlling the masses, Henry believed that one should attempt to counter notions of 'imposed' leisure by promoting notions of 'guided' leisure. By guided leisure Henry meant the formulation of projects which would contribute to the development of the person. Crucial to this was the need to reassert the unity between work and leisure, two spheres which were coming more and more to be seen as separate. For Henry, in order to become a complete person, leisure must not be 'empty time', nor should work be an activity in which people felt exploited and dissatisfied, and from which they longed to escape into 'empty time':

> In fact whoever abandons the attempt to assimilate one part of his life destroys his life. Leisure which is only a compensation for work that is deprived of human meaning and devoid of all substance is an impoverished form of leisure, However, leisure will take on its full value if, when he is resting, the worker's thoughts are rooted in a life in which nothing is relegated to one side, in which all the experience of work brings its own richness to the construction of a human life which transcends work, but which does not repudiate it.[9]

In this and related passages in the Henry article we find a typically personalist mixture of politics and spirituality. On the one hand, there is an implicit demand for a change in social and political structures which would make work into a non-exploited, fully human and personal area of life, and on the other hand, there is a call for the development of true spirituality in each person, without which there can be no meaning. This dual perspective of the political and the spiritual was one which was distinctively personalist and one to which Mounier held tenaciously.

Mounier's attraction to the Pascalian notion of *divertissement* was always strong, as can be seen in this passage from his work *Le Personnalisme*, in which this notion determines much of his thinking about leisure.

The man of diversion [*l'homme du divertissement*] lives as if expelled from the self, merged in the external commotion: like the man who is prisoner of his appetites, functions, habits, relationships and of the world that distracts him. Instantaneous life, no memory, no project, no control which is the very definition of exteriority . . . .

Personal life begins with the capacity to break with one's surroundings, to take a grip of oneself . . . in order to gather oneself together around a centre, to unify oneself. At first this movement appears to be a movement of withdrawal. But this withdrawal is only a first step in a more complex movement. If some people stop there and contort themselves at this stage then a perversion has taken place. It is not the withdrawal which is important, but the concentration, the *conversion* of energy. The person steps back only in order to take a better leap forward. It is on this vital experience that the values of silence and retreat are founded. It is timely to recall them today. The distractions of our civilisation eat away at the meaning of leisure, at the fondness for time that passes slowly, at the patience needed for a work to mature, and these distractions disperse those interior voices which soon will only be listened to by the poet and the religious man.[10]

Here Mounier begins by drawing a strict distinction between exteriority and interiority. The man who diverts himself is expelled from his inner self and loses himself in the mass. But true personal life only begins when one breaks with one's surroundings, collects oneself together and retains one's centre and inner unity. Mounier then goes on to deny that withdrawal and turning in on the self can be a permanently healthy and desirable state for the modern person. Withdrawal and concentration are the necessary springboards for returning to the world with the requisite energy and spirituality.

Mounier insists that he wants to avoid a rather self-indulgent notion of interiority:

> True interiority essential to personal life has become a form of devitalised spirituality, masquerading under the notion of 'inner life', a form of decadent self-indulgence. It is nothing but the individual turning in on himself and his own complexities, all of which are the result of luxury and idleness. This situation has reached such a point that some people think that spiritual life is inseparable from bourgeois leisure.[11]

Mounier wanted to move towards more strenuous notions of leisure, based on a different conception of contemplation and interiority. For him, contemplation, silence and rest went together, not with ease and self-indulgence, but with self-examination, metaphysical anxiety, spiritual inquiry and moral protest.[12]

Personalism was a philosophy developed in the 1930s whose aim was to protect the freedom of the person in a context of rising fascism and totalitarianism. But, equally, personalism was a philosophy which aimed to protect the person against the capitalist society of leisure and consumerism. This dimension of personalism, though present in the earliest texts, became gradually more and more important. In postwar society, as prosperity began to bring about swift and radical changes, Mounier's preoccupation with consumer society became central. Whereas mass society in the 1930s seems mainly to have evoked the spectres of fascism and totalitarianism, in the 1940s and 1950s mass society came more and more to mean mass consumer society, with its mechanised industry, its mass means of communication and its mass forms of leisure. Several passages in Mounier's early text of the 1930s, *Révolution personnaliste et communautaire,* make clear his attitude to mass culture and mass leisure:

> One sees that it is not only a matter of 'occupying leisure time', as the impoverished political formula has it, but of giving leisure a meaning and direction which is a very different thing. Depending on the choice we make, mechanisation will bring us a world of petty bourgeois with full bellies, or a world of men free at last for most of the day to lift up their heads to partake in mystical debates and truly human activities.[13]

In the past even entertainment [*divertissement*] was something to be conquered: now with wireless, records and sporting events, the man who distracts himself is a spectator. . . . The cinema is the spiritual daily bread of the crowds, and when it is not emptying the mind, it is accustoming the imagination to strong visual experiences, and for this reason blunts it all the more and leaves it powerless in the face of a life which offers neither close-ups, nor special effects, nor those insistent visual explanations of people's souls.[14]

The rush of money and the quiet life. A type of hollow man – fortunately he resists, the blighter! – devoid of all madness, of all mystery, of all sense of being and of love, of suffering and of Joy, dedicated to Happiness and Security; in the higher classes he has a veneer of Politeness, Good Humour and Aristocratic Virtues; in the lower classes he is hemmed in between the sluggish reading of the daily newspaper, wage claims and the boredom of Sundays and bank holidays, and with only the latest popular song and the latest scandal to turn to as a form of escape. When one has described the star's eyebrows, little amusing toys like the yo-yo, and pastimes like crosswords . . . one has described in full the spiritual bourgeois person.[15]

Mounier is particularly contemptuous of the twin ideals of modern consumer society – 'happiness and security'. These he takes to be representative of a petty bourgeois mentality now rapidly being adopted by all classes ('the city of the future will be one in which one will be able to eat one's fill and go to the cinema every evening').[16] According to Mounier, however, the modern committed intellectual cannot allow himself to go along with the mass. His mission is to bear witness to present injustices and corruption. The true 'person' must perform this necessary moral task on a daily basis. He must permanently serve the truth, and must not be seduced into the new consumer and leisure culture:

The task of denunciation and desolidarisation, which we are trying to pursue here, everyone can do the same in his daily life. One needs more courage than one might think: to whistle at a film when the audience is mute with indifference; to single out a dubious expression that everybody accepts; to struggle ceaselessly against the silence and indifference which makes up the cosy atmosphere of a culture based on lies. 'We must create a militia of truth', a friend wrote to me, 'an invisible loyal militia'. As another friend wrote to me, however disagreeable it may be, and however dangerous it may be to persist in such a line of behaviour, we have to agree to be the discordant note.[17]

Daily life must not be an 'acquiescence' in the new materialistic culture of ease and comfort.[18] The true person for Mounier appears to be one who is taut and ungiving, someone who devotes himself unflinchingly and constantly to the moral task of refusing the present state of society and of working to bring into being the future good society.[19] This essentially 'militant' attitude seems least likely to promote a desire for leisure. In fact, it leads precisely to a refusal of leisure ('we must be present at the suffering of the world. We do not have the right to withdraw into leisure').[20] This refusal of leisure on the part of French intellectuals of the mid-century can be seen in part as a reaction against the cultural life of the 1920s which Mounier saw as having given itself up to the folly of incessant play.[21] From the 1930s to well into the 1960s French intellectual life was marked by this rejection of hedonism and by the dominance of notions of sacrifice and commitment among writers and intellectuals, whether they were Christians, Marxists, Existentialists, Humanists, or indeed any combination of these.

The great irony of this 'heroic' refusal of mass leisure is that, although most progressive French intellectuals profoundly desired to 'serve the people', they were in reality unable to 'join' them, since they saw them on the whole as being simply passive victims of the new leisure industry. Mounier had an obvious contempt and distaste for the modern forms of popular leisure as they actually existed: sport, music, dancing, cinema, and the rest. He could only see in them evidence of spiritual waste, and of irresponsible diversion from the truly important social, political and indeed spiritual questions of the day. What is more, they were for him quintessential activities of 'the mass' and hence were taken by him to be signs of submission to authority and of escape into complacency and security. For Mounier, therefore, the true act of personal liberty was to refuse mass leisure, and thereby to refuse false communion with the people in their leisure.[22]

If Mounier was deeply suspicious of leisure under capitalism, he was also suspicious of the democratic socialist attempts to regulate and humanise modern consumer society. This is clear in one of his last texts, *Du Bonheur*, an essay on the condition of postwar Sweden. This work is a kind of 'air-conditioned nightmare' text, for Mounier sees in Sweden a 'Scandinavian America', and a prototype of the city of the future.[23] For Mounier, Sweden is a land of economic prosperity, social peace and order, but it is also a land of spiritual poverty. Mounier seems above all to react against 'the mystique of organisation', which he says even invades those moments when one should be spontaneous.

> Advent is waged like a propaganda campaign (the calendar on which each day one opens a window; the candlesticks on which each Sunday one lights a candle; the Christmas tree that has been planned since the 20th of November). May Day resembles a military exercise and is the signal for summer clothes – not a week earlier, not a week later.[24]

Swedish life is too mechanical, too hygienic and too communal for Mounier's taste. In their leisure activities the Swedes seem to Mounier to be desperately escaping from solitariness. Only this, he says, can explain their 'frantic need to join clubs and societies'.[25] He claims that the Swedes set up a society for every possible activity, and rather surprisingly he seems to be criticising them for their earnestness, as when he highlights the enormous popularity of adult education and evening classes in Sweden. According to Mounier, the Swedes prefer to educate themselves in their leisure time, rather than drink the quota of three litres of alchohol which the state grants them each month. The mechanical, regulated and planned world of leisure, in which it is believed that happiness can be organised and guaranteed, is for Mounier an illusion, for he believes that Sweden proves that prosperity and security end by depriving people of the essentials, which are energy, spontaneity, creativity and spirituality. A space for leisure can be staked out and fully equipped, and time can be generously allotted to play there, but Mounier obviously believes that in such conditions man either does not want to play or that the play is sterile.[26]

In the contemporary state of society and in the society of the future, as foreshadowed in the example of Sweden, Mounier could see no way in which the heroic intellectual, the true person, could participate in the leisure activities of his fellow men. This, however, can be seen as a considerable contradiction of essential elements of Mounier's personalist philosophy, for Mounier also saw the limitations in the stance of one who chose to maintain a moral distance from the mass of the people. Mounier criticised 'this state of tension in the individual which renders him opaque and closed to others and to new experiences'. He also maintained that liberty is not only 'refusal' and 'rupture':

The movement towards freedom is also allowing oneself to relax, to be permeable, to be open to others and to new experiences. It is not only a question of rupture and conquest, it is also and ultimately a question of being able to connect.[27]

For Mounier, one of the highest forms of experience for the person was that of 'transpersonalisation' – true communion with other persons. In the mass society in which he found himself and which he saw as more and more the face of the future society, Mounier did not, however, believe that 'a full personal community' was possible, except on the level of small elite groups of like-minded persons, groups in which respect for others would be guaranteed.[28] For this reason he also tended to look back nostalgically at times when he believed that communities did exist that allowed people to participate in fully human forms of leisure. Equally, he looked forward in a utopian way to a possible revival of such authentic communal leisure forms:

Let peasants again feel the desire to celebrate with dances, songs, performances, festivals of the land; let workers desire and create beautiful factories; let faith rid itself of the favours of decadent piety, and let it once again learn how to proclaim itself in song and in images.[29]

According to Mounier, art and culture could play the crucial role in raising the level of people's leisure activities, in making them truly meaningful and in bringing people together in a genuine form of communion. Mounier, therefore, like so many of the *animateurs* in postwar France, tended to think that leisure time ought to be taken up by people seeking out challenging aesthetic experiences. Such experiences would not only sharpen their moral awareness but would face them with a contrary message to the one promoted by capitalist society. The austere men of Mounier's generation did not want people to believe in the possibility of material happiness and material security in this world. In order to be a complete person one had to be willing to face the inexorable realities of injustice, suffering and death, all of which the modern leisure industry was designed to mask. For Mounier, therefore, leisure had to offer the possibility of genuine communion with other persons, and communion which would not principally aim for 'happiness' since happiness was not for him the ultimate value. To be true to the self and to the human condition, 'leisure time' would also have to recognise man's permanent and profound sense of 'dissatisfaction' and 'anxiety'.

Mounier often attacked modern forms of Jansenism and believed he escaped such austere and unworldly forms of religion.[30] However, an examination of Mounier's views on leisure shows that he is close to a 'Jansenist' position in so far as leisure in modern society was for him still seen as 'diversion', 'agitation without purpose' and 'idleness'. Leisure was also the natural concomitant of 'abundance', 'luxury' and 'comfort'. But it is true to say that Mounier did not follow a pure Jansenist line in so far as he did not believe that each person needed to find his salvation in solitariness. In fact, Mounier disapproved of modern leisure because it failed to offer the possibility of achieving the desired balance between the person and the community. The ideal for Mounier was that when persons come together in leisure they should do so in full recognition of the humanity of each other person. Indeed, this coming together in leisure should be precisely the privileged moment in which persons learn how to be members of the community, to respect other persons, while fully remaining persons in their own right:

Learning how to live in a community is learning how to relate to one's neighbour, as one person to another person, which has been called, rather felicitously, learning to treat the other as 'thou'.

It is no longer a question of looking for spontaneous pleasure, or the diversion of being together while each one distracts himself from the other. Depersonalised individuals, strangers to each other, still enjoy being together, either to find themselves in each other, or to occupy their souls left vacant by curiosity, irritation and the fragile drama of the differences that separate them. . . .

The 'us' of these gatherings is always an 'other' us. Everyone is distracted from the self; the collection of people is also as if alienated from itself. Everyone uses the other in front of him as a receptacle from which he can draw something, or in which he can throw away something, or with which he can play, or on which he can play tricks. The other is still for him a 'third person', a 'him', that is to say a thing, any old bit of something which has no value of its own and which can be changed for something else. The soldier in line, the party member for the politician, the woman with whom one flirts.[31]

The tradition of French writing on leisure, which I evoked at the beginning of this study, and which I said ran from the 1930s to the 1960s, was in a large part a 'humanism of leisure'.[32] It stressed the predominant need for civic awareness and social responsibility within leisure. Mounier played a significant role in this 'humanism of leisure' by his consistent stress on the need for unyielding moral seriousness and communal responsibility within leisure time. Mounier, however, added his own particular dimension to the 'communalism' of leisure, by his insistence that a true balance needed to be found between the 'personal' and the 'communitarian'. Mounier sought to achieve a dynamic, symbiotic relationship, in which both the community of persons and each separate person profited from the mutual respect accorded to each other, and without which neither the person nor the community of persons could achieve what Mounier always saw as the aim of personalism – the full spiritual blossoming of each person and the community at large.

Notes

1. Joffre Dumazedier's works, and especially *Vers une civilisation du loisir* (1962), are central to this tradition and in a sense bring it to a culminating point.
2. In the writings of Dumazedier and other affiliated writers on leisure, the words 'culture' and 'leisure' are very intimately linked, and are often even interchangeable.
3. See E. Ritaine, *Les Stratèges de la culture* (Paris 1983).
4. J. Charpentreau and L. Rocher, *L'Esthétique personnaliste d'Emmanuel Mounier* (Paris, 1966) pp. 126–7.
5. F. Henry, 'Loisirs et personne humaine', in *La Personne humaine en péril*, Semaines sociales de France, Clermont-Ferrand, XXIXe Session, 1937 (Lyon, 1938).
6. Ibid., p. 487.
7. Ibid., p. 481.
8. Ibid., p. 483.
9. Ibid., pp. 486–7.
10. E. Mounier, *Oeuvres*, vol. iii: *1944–1950* (Paris, 1962) pp. 462–3.
11. Ibid., pp. 211–12.
12. Ibid., pp. 213.
13. E. Mounier, *Oeuvres*, vol. i: *1931–1939* (Paris, 1961) p. 413.
14. Ibid., pp. 155–6.
15. Ibid., p. 179.
16. Mounier, *Oeuvres,* vol. iii, p. 336.
17. Ibid., p. 341.
18. Mounier, *Oeuvres,* vol. i, p. 355.
19. Ibid., p. 141.
20. Ibid., pp. 342–3.
21. Ibid., pp.130–1.
22. Mounier, *Oeuvres*, vol. iii, p. 482.

23. E. Mounier, *Oeuvres*, vol. IV: *Recueils posthumes, correspondance* (Paris, 1963) pp. 273, 276.
24. Ibid., p. 274.
25. Ibid., p. 262. Mounier seems always to have had this scathing attitude to clubs, which is rather surprising, given the importance of 'associations' for those postwar cultural *animateurs* who were also followers of Mounier. The following is a typical early expression of Mounier's antipathy to clubs and associations:

> We will not be taken in by the apparent proliferation of community organisations . . . . On the surface there have never been so many 'communities' . . . .: the couple, the family, the trade association, the union, the nation, the electoral body, political parties, religious denominations, let us not forget Europe, the S.D.N. and the numberless associations for which anyone can receive a stamped card, depending on among other things whether he has dabbled in fishing, general ideas or board games.
>
> There have never been so many societies. Never has there been so little community. (Mounier, *Oeuvres,* vol. I, p. 185)

26. Mounier, *Oeuvres*, vol. IV, p. 276.
27. *Oeuvres*, vol. III, p. 484.
28. 'At least in our present context, this can hardly be attained except in groups of two or in groups of a very small number of persons: couple, closest friend, small group of friends, loyal companions, militants' (ibid., p. 459).
29. Mounier, *Oeuvres*, vol. I, p. 266.
30. Ibid., pp. 256, 278.
31. Ibid., p. 192.
32. The term is Dumazedier's in *Esprit,* no. 274 (June 1959) p. 893. This issue of *Esprit* is devoted to leisure.

Index